Reading
Voca
for
IELTS

Reading Voca for IELTS

발행일	2019년 3월 22일		
지은이	전현선		
펴낸이	손형국		
펴낸곳	(주)북랩		
편집인	선일영	편집	오경진, 권혁신, 최승헌, 최예은, 김경무
디자인	이현수, 김민하, 한수희, 김윤주, 허지혜	제작	박기성, 황동현, 구성우, 정성배
마케팅	김회란, 박진관, 조하라		
출판등록	2004. 12. 1(제2012-000051호)		
주소	서울시 금천구 가산디지털 1로 168, 우림라이온스밸리 B동 B113, 114호		
홈페이지	www.book.co.kr		
전화번호	(02)2026-5777	팩스	(02)2026-5747
ISBN	979-11-6299-570-9 13740 (종이책)		979-11-6299-571-6 15740 (전자책)

이 도서의 국립중앙도서관 출판예정도서목록(CIP)은 서지정보유통지원시스템 홈페이지(http://seoji.nl.go.kr)와
국가자료공동목록시스템(http://www.nl.go.kr/kolisnet)에서 이용하실 수 있습니다.
(CIP제어번호: CIP2019009684)

IELTS 고득점으로 가기 위한 필수 어휘 훈련서

Reading Voca for IELTS

전현선 지음

북랩 book Lab

PREFACE

기존에 나와 있는 VOCA 교재는 양이 방대해서 접근하기 쉽지 않습니다. 이 교재는 『Cambridge IELTS』를 쉽게 공부할 수 있도록 순서대로 문맥에 맞게 의미를 담았기 때문에 Reading 공부에 많은 도움이 될 것으로 생각합니다.

이 교재로 공부하실 때 단어를 단어 자체로 외우기보다 Reading Passage를 읽어 가면서 의미 파악을 하는 방법이 효율적입니다. REVIEW 부분의 공란은 각각의 의미가 있습니다. Reading뿐만 아니라 Writing에서 유용하게 쓰이는 단어나 구문은 영어 부분에 공란을 두었고 의미만 파악해도 되는 단어는 한글에 공란을 남겼습니다.

많은 도움이 되었으면 하는 바람입니다. 감사합니다.

2019년 3월
전현선

CONTENTS

PART 02 Cambridge IELTS 13

Cambridge IELTS 12

TEST

5

Cork

VOCA

Paragraph 1

cork	코르크, 마개
the thick bark of ~	~의 두꺼운 껍질
a remarkable material	놀라운 물질
tough, elastic, buoyant and fire-resistant	거친, 탄력 있는, 부력 있는 그리고 내화성의
be suitable for ~	~에 적합한
a wide rage of purposes	다양한 목적들
for millennia	천년 동안
the ancient Egyptians	고대의 이집트인들은
seal A with B	A를 B로 봉하다
beehive	벌집, 벌통

Paragraph 2

itself	그 자체
an extraordinary tree	특별한 나무
in thickness	두께에 있어서
insulate	보온하다, 단열하다
the trunk and branches	몸통과 나뭇가지
constant	일정한
all year round	일 년 내내
most probably	아마도
as a defence against forest fires	산불에 대한 방어로서
a cellular structure	세포 구조
per cubic centimetre	세제곱미터당
succeed in replicating	복제에서 성공하다
be filled with ~	~로 가득 차다
, which is why	그것은 이유이다
elasticity	탄력성
squash it and watch it	그것을 짓누르고 그것을 보다
spring back to ~	~로 돌아가다
release the pressure	압력을 풀다

Paragraph 3

a number of Mediterranean countries	많은 지중해 국가들
flourish	번창하다
a minimum of ~	최소 ~
not more than	단지, 고작
grape vines	포도 덩굴들
thrive in poor soil	나쁜 토양에서 성장하다(번창하다)
put down deep roots	뿌리를 깊게 내리다
in search of ~	~을 찾아서
moisture and nutrients	수분과 영양분들
region	지역
meet all of requirements	모든 요건들을 충족하다
account for roughly half of ~	대략 ~의 반을 차지하다

Paragraph 4

family-owned	가족 소유의
above all	무엇보다도
exercise in patience	인내심을 발휘하다
from A to B	A에서 B까지
a sapling	어린 나무
the first harvest	첫 수확
a gap of approximately a decade	대략 10년의 차이
separate A from B	A를 B로부터 분리하다
top-quality	최상 등급의
be stripped	벗겨지다
damp	습기가 있는
a very specialized profession	전문화된 직업
medical means	의료적 수단
invent	개발하다
highly skilled workers	아주 기술 있는 노동자
vertical cuts	수직 절단
sharp axes	뾰족한 도끼들
lever it away in pieces	조각조각 지렛대로 옮기다
as large as they can manage	그들이 관리할 수 있을 정도로 크게
prise away a semi-circular husk	반원형의 껍질을 비틀다
from above ground level to first branches	지면 위로부터 첫 번째 가지까지
on the ground	바닥에서
be taken to factories	공장으로 옮겨지다
boil to kill any insects	벌레를 죽이기 위해 끓이다

traditional bottle stoppers	전통적인 병뚜껑들
most of the remainder being used	남아 있는 대부분은 사용되다
in the construction trade	건축 관계 일에
be ideal for ~	~에 이상적이다
thermal and acoustic insulation	열과 소리의 단열
granules of cork	코르크의 밀 입자
the manufacture of concrete	콘크리트 제조

Paragraph 5

the end of the virtual monopoly	사실상 독점의 한계
due to concerns about the effect	영향에 대한 염려 때문에
the contents of the bottle	병의 내용물
caused by a chemical compound	화학적 화합물에 의해 야기된
the tiniest concentrations	가장 작은 농도
as little as ~	~만큼 적은
trillion	1조
spoil the taste of product	상품의 맛을 상하게 하다
a gradual yet steady move toward ~	서서히 그러나 꾸준히 ~쪽으로 움직이다
screw caps	나사 마개들
substitutes	대체품들
manufacture	제조하다, 만들다
in the case of ~	~의 경우에
convenient for the user	사용자에게 편리한

Paragraph 6

several advantages	몇 가지 장점들
the type of high quality goods	높은 수준의 상품 종류들
has long been associated	오랫동안 관련되어 오다
a sustainable product	지속 가능한 상품
be recycled without difficulty	어려움 없이 재활용되다
local biodiversity	지역 생물의 다양성
prevent desertification	사막화를 막다
given the current concerns about ~	현재의 ~에 대한 근심을 감안할 때
environmental issues	환경적인 문제들
ancient material	오래된 물질
look promising	전망 있는 것 같다

REVIEW

Paragraph 1

cork	
the thick bark of ~	
	놀라운 물질
tough, elastic, buoyant and fire-resistant	
	~에 적합한
	다양한 목적들
for millennia	
the ancient Egyptians	
seal A with B	
beehive	

Paragraph 2

itself	
	특별한 나무
in thickness	
	보온하다, 단열하다
the trunk and branches	
	일정한
	일 년 내내
	아마도
as a defence against forest fires	
a cellular structure	
per cubic centimetre	세제곱미터당
succeed in replicating	
	~로 가득 차다
, which is why	
	탄력성
squash it and watch it	
spring back to ~	
	압력을 풀다

Paragraph 3

a number of Mediterranean countries	
	번창하다
a minimum of ~	

	단지, 고작
	포도 덩굴들
thrive in poor soil	
put down deep roots	
	~을 찾아서
moisture and nutrients	
	지역
meet all of requirements	
account for roughly half of ~	

Paragraph 4

	가족 소유의
	무엇보다도
	인내심을 발휘하다
	A로부터 B까지
a sapling	
the first harvest	
a gap of approximately a decade	
	A를 B로부터 분리하다
top-quality	
be stripped	
damp	
	전문화된 직업
	의료적 수단
	개발하다
	아주 기술 있는 노동자
vertical cuts	
sharp axes	
lever it away in pieces	
as large as they can manage	
prise away a semi-circular husk	
from above ground level to first branches	
on the ground	
	공장으로 옮겨지다
boil to kill any insects	
traditional bottle stoppers	
most of the remainder being used	
in the construction trade	
	~에 이상적이다
thermal and acoustic insulation	

granules of cork	
the manufacture of concrete	

Paragraph 5

the end of the virtual monopoly	
	영향에 대한 염려 때문에
the contents of the bottle	
caused by a chemical compound	
the tiniest concentrations	
as little as	
	1조
spoil the taste of product	
a gradual yet steady move toward ~	
screw caps	
	대체품들
	제조하다, 만들다
	~의 경우에
	사용자에게 편리한

Paragraph 6

	몇 가지 장점들
the type of high quality goods	
has long been associated	
	지속 가능한 상품
	어려움 없이 재활용되다
	지역 생물의 다양성
	사막화를 막다
	현재의 ~에 대한 근심을 감안할 때
	환경적인 문제들
	오래된 물질
	전망 있는 것 같다

PASSAGE 2
COLLECTING AS A HOBBY

VOCA

Paragraph 1

collecting	수집
the most varied of human activities	가장 다양한 인간 활동들
psychologist	심리학자, 정신과 의사
fascinating	재미있는, 매혹적인
be dignified with ~	~으로 위엄이 갖춰지다
a technical name	학명
postage stamps	우표들
amassing	모으는 것
wrappers or whatever	포장지 또는 무엇이든지
put to use	사용하다
much more productive	훨씬 더 생산적인
and yet	그런데도
millions of collectors	수백만의 수집가들

Paragraph 2

make money	돈을 벌다
an instrumental reason for ~	~에 대한 중요한(도구적) 이유
that is	즉, 다시 말해서
as a means to an end	목적을 위한 수단으로서
look for antiques	골동품들을 찾다
sell at a profit	이익을 내서 팔다
may well	당연하다
psychological element	심리적 요소
sell dear	비싸게 팔다
a sense of triumph	승리감

Paragraph 3

develop social life	사회생활을 발전시키다
attend meetings	모임에 참여하다
exchange information on items	물품에 대한 정보를 나누다

a variant on ~	~에 대한 변종
join a bridge club	브리지 클럽에 가입하다
bring into contact with ~	~와 접촉을 가져오다
like-minded people	마음이 맞는 사람들

Paragraph 4

another motive	또 다른 동기
the desire to find something special	특별한 어떤 것을 찾고자 하는 바람
a rare early recording	희귀 초반 녹음
hunt for ~	~를 찾는 사냥
give a purpose to a life	삶에 목적을 주다
otherwise	그렇지 않으면
feel aimless	목적이 없다고 느끼다
be lucky enough to ~	~ 할 정도로 충분히 행운이다
rather than celebrating their success	그들의 성공을 축하하는 것보다
feel empty	공허함을 느끼다
now that ~	~때문에

Paragraph 5

potential reason for ~	~에 대한 잠재적인 이유
a result of ~	~의 결과
educational value	교육적인 가치
open a window to ~	~을 받아들이다
amass fossils	화석을 모으다
a vast amount of information	엄청난 정보
be greatly inferior to ~	~보다 뒤지다(열등하다)

Paragraph 6

in the past	과거에
to a lesser extent	보다 적게
a popular form of collecting	수집의 인기 있는 형태
trainspotting	기관차 번호를 기록하기
involve	관련되다
locomotive	기관차
published data	발표된 정보들
identify	확인하다, 알아보다
tick off	확인하다, 알리다
transpotters	기차 탐색자들
work out	해결하다
as a byproduct	부산물로서

practitioners of hobby	취미를 실천하는 사람들
become very knowledgeable about ~	~에 대해 정통하게 되다
railway operations	철도 작동들
technical specifications	전문적인 세부 사항들

Paragraph 7

similarly	비슷하게도
go beyond	능가하다, 범위를 넘다
enlarge their collection	그들의 수집을 확대하다
develop an interest in the way	방법에 있어서 관심사를 발전시키다
materials	물질들
over centuries	수 세기에 걸쳐서
the wax and porcelain	밀랍과 자기
be inspired to study	공부하도록 자극받다
reflect notions	개념(생각)을 보여 주다(반영하다)
ought to	해야만 하다

Paragraph 8

not all collectors are interested in ~	모든 수집가들이 ~에 관심이 있는 것은 아니다
a sense of control	통제력
as a way of dealing with insecurity	불안정을 다루는 방법으로서
arrange neatly	깔끔하게 배치하다, 정리하다
organize their collection	그들의 수집을 정리하다
according to certain commonplace principles	일정한 일반적인 원칙에 따라
depict	묘사하다, 표현하다

Paragraph 9

conscious or not	의식적이든 아니든
individualism	개인주의
as unexpected as ~	~처럼 예상 밖의
convey their belief	그들의 믿음을 전달하다
believe it or not	믿기 힘들겠지만 (이것은 사실이다)
at least	적어도
in existence	현존하는
grow out of a personal collection	개인적 수집으로부터 성장한다

Paragraph 10

the common factor	공통된 요인
passion	열정
mildly	가볍게

more than ~	~보다, ~ 이상으로
totally engrossing	완전히 마음을 사로잡는
a strong sense of personal fulfilment	강한 개인적 성취감
non-collectors	비수집가들
appear an eccentric	기이한 것 같다
if harmless	만약에 해가 안 되면
potentially	잠재적으로
has a lot going for it	유리한 점이 많다

REVIEW

Paragraph 1

	수집
the most varied of human activities	
	심리학자, 정신과 의사
	재미있는, 매혹적인
	~으로 위엄이 갖춰지다
	학명
	우표들
	모으는 것
	포장지 또는 무엇이든지
put to use	
much more productive	
and yet	
millions of collectors	

Paragraph 2

	돈을 벌다
an instrumental reason for ~	
	즉, 다시 말해서
as a means to an end	
	골동품들을 찾다
	이익을 내서 팔다
	당연하다
	심리적 요소
	비싸게 팔다
	승리감

Paragraph 3

	사회생활을 발전시키다
	모임에 참여하다
	물품에 대한 정보를 나누다
a variant on	
join a bridge club	
bring into contact with ~	
	마음이 맞는 사람들

Paragraph 4

	또 다른 동기
the desire to find something special	
a rare early recording	
	~를 찾는 사냥
	삶에 목적을 주다
	그렇지 않으면
	목적이 없다고 느끼다
	~ 할 정도로 충분히 행운이다
	그들의 성공을 축하하는 것보다
	공허함을 느끼다
	~ 때문에

Paragraph 5

	~에 대한 잠재적인 이유
	교육적인 가치
	~을 받아들이다
	화석을 모으다
	엄청난 정보
	~보다 뒤지다(열등하다)

Paragraph 6

	과거에
	보다 적게
a popular form of collecting	
trainspotting	
	관련되다
	기관차
published data	발표된 정보들
	확인하다, 알아보다
	확인하다, 알리다
transpotters	
	해결하다
	부산물로서
practitioners of hobby	
become very knowledgeable about ~	
railway operations	
technical specifications	

Paragraph 7

	비슷하게도
	능가하다, 범위를 넘다
enlarge their collection	
develop an interest in the way	
	물질들
	수 세기에 걸쳐서
the wax and porcelain	
	공부하도록 자극받다
	개념(생각)을 보여 주다(반영하다)
ought to	

Paragraph 8

not all collectors are interested in ~	
	통제력
as a way of dealing with insecurity	
	깔끔하게 배치하다, 정리하다
	그들의 수집을 정리하다
according to certain commonplace principles	
depict	

Paragraph 9

	의식적이든 아니든
	개인주의
	~처럼 예상 밖의
	그들의 믿음을 전달하다
	믿기 힘들겠지만 (이것은 사실이다)
	적어도
	현존하는
grow out of a personal collection	

Paragraph 10

	공통된 요인
	열정
	가볍게
	~보다, ~ 이상으로
	완전히 마음을 사로잡는
a strong sense of personal fulfillment	
	비수집가들

	기이한 것 같다
	만약에 해가 안 되면
	잠재적으로
has a lot going for it	

PASSAGE 3
What's the purpose of gaining knowledge?

VOCA

Paragraph A

found an institution	기관을 설립하다
instruction	교육
subject	과목
the founder' motto	설립자의 방침(표어)
an apt characterization	적절한 특성
currently	최근의
philosophy	철학, 이론
prepare for a career	직업을 준비하다
resort management	리조트 관리
accounting	회계
law enforcement	법의 집행
you name it	그 밖에 무엇이든지
Arson for Profit	이익을 위한 방화
I kid you not	농담이 아니야, 정말이야
undergraduates	학부생들
meet the academic requirements	학문적 요구를 충족하다
sing up for ~	~을 신청하다

Paragraph B

naturally	자연스럽게
be intended for	~을 위해 의도되다
prospective arson investigators	유망한 화재 수사관들
the tricks of the trade	일에 대한 수법들
detect if ~	~인지 아닌지 감지하다
be desperately set	의도적으로 붙여지다
discover who did it	누가 그것을 했는지 발견하다
establish a chain of evidence	일련의 증거를 밝히다(규명하다)
effective prosecution	효율적인 기소(고발)
in a court of law	법정에서
prospective arsonists	잠재적인 방화범들

be highly welcome	아주 환영받다
criticize	비판하다
the increasing professionalization of ~	~에 대한 증가하는 전문화
occupations	직업들
it is not unknown	잘 알려져 있다
a firefighter	소방관
torch a building	건물을 불태우다
dishonest and illegal behaviour	부정직하고 불법적인 행동
with the help of higher education	고등 교육의 도움으로
creep into every aspect	모든 면에 영향을 주다
public and business life	공적이고 사업적인 생활

Paragraph C

anew	새로이
a class in marketing	마케팅 강의
degree programs	학위 프로그램
the regular instructor	정규 교사(강사)
a colleague	동료
appreciate	인정하다, 알아주다
the kind of ethical perspective	일종의 도덕적 관점
as a philosopher	철학자로서
endless ways	무한한 방법들
approach this assignment	연구 과제에 접근하다
take my cue from ~	~부터 힌트를 얻다
Principles of Marketing	경영의 원리
make me think	내가 생각하게 하다
principled	도덕적인, 윤리적인
after all	어쨌든
a subject matter	과목의 문제
being codified	성문화되다
in the sense of being ethical	도덕적이 되는 측면에서
assume	가정하다, 추측하다
the answer to ~	~에 대한 대답
marketing principles	마케팅 원리
obvious	분명한
look at the ways	방식들을 보다
everything under the sun	천지만물
in a ethical(principled) fashion	윤리적인 면으로

Paragraph D

make the suggestion	제안을 하다
sound downright crazy	완전히 미친 소리로 들리다
in light of the evidence	증거 측면에서
by definition	정의상
be principled	윤리적이다
inspiration for the judgment	판단에 대한 원천
philosopher	철학자
argue	주장하다
any body of knowledge	지식의 본문
consist of ~	~로 구성하다
an end and a means	목적과 수단

Paragraph E

apply A to B	A를 B에 적용하다
in order to ~	~ 하기 위해서
how to market effectively	어떻게 효율적으로 판매하는지
to what end	무엇 때문에
two main attitudes toward ~	~에 대한 두 가지 주요한 태도들
the purposed of ~	~의 목적
make money	돈을 벌다
irrelevant	전혀 무관한, 무의미한
the acquisition of ~	~의 습득
marketing expertise	마케팅 전문 지식
as such	그렇게
proposal	제안
neither of ~	~의 둘 다 아니다
capture the significance of the end	목적에 대한 중요성을 파악하다
a field of knowledge	지식 분야
a professional endeavor	전문적인 노력
be defined by ~	~에 의해 정의되다
hence	따라서
deserve scrutiny	면밀히 조사할 만하다

Paragraph F

at this point	이 시점에서
becomes supremely relevant	매우 관련 있게 되다
presumably	아마도
all about means	수단에 관한 모든 것

how to detect and prosecute	어떻게 탐지하고 기소하는지
criminal activity	범죄자 활동
therefore	그러므로
in an ethical sense	도덕적 의미에서
ask A to B	A에게 B를 묻다
articulate the end or purpose	목적 또는 의도를 분명히 하다
eventually	결국에
generalize to ~	~로 일반화하다
The safety and welfare of society	사회의 안전과 복지
the very same knowledge of means	수단에 대한 동일한 지식
achieve a much less noble end	훨씬 덜 고귀한 목적을 달성하다
such as personal profit	개인적 이익과 같은
via destructive, dangerous, reckless activity	파괴적인, 위험한, 무모한 행동을 통해서
firefighting	소방, 소방 활동
a seperate word	별개의 단어
arson	방화
similarly	비슷하게도
employ	이용하다
the principles of marketing	마케팅의 원리
in an unprincipled way	비윤리적인 방법에 있어서
term for it	그것에 대한 용어
fraud	사기
the example of a doctor and a poisoner	의사와 독살자의 예
identical knowledge	똑같은 지식
divergent ends	서로 다른 목적들
practice medicine	의료업에 종사하다
murder	살인자

REVIEW

Paragraph A

found an institution	
instruction	
	과목
the founder' motto	
an apt characterization	
	최근의
	철학, 이론
prepare for a career	
resort management	
	회계
	법의 집행
you name it	
Arson for Profit	
	학부생들
meet the academic requirements	
	~을 신청하다

Paragraph B

	자연스럽게
be intended for	
prospective arson investigators	
the tricks of the trade	
	~인지 아닌지 감지하다
be desperately set	
discover who did it	
establish a chain of evidence	
effective prosecution	
in a court of law	
prospective arsonists	
be highly welcome	
	비판하다
the increasing professionalization of ~	
	직업들
	잘 알려져 있다
	소방관

torch a building	
dishonest and illegal behaviour	
with the help of higher education	
creep into every aspect	
public and business life	

Paragraph C

anew	
a class in marketing	
degree programs	
the regular instructor	
	동료
appreciate	
the kind of ethical perspective	
as a philosopher	
endless ways	
approach this assignment	
take my cue from ~	
Principles of Marketing	
	내가 생각하게 하다
principled	
	어쨌든
a subject matter	
being codified	
in the sense of being ethical	
assume	
the answer to ~	
marketing principles	
	분명한
look at the ways	
everything under the sun	
in a ethical(principled) fashion	

Paragraph D

make the suggestion	
sound downright crazy	
in light of the evidence	
	정의상
be principled	
inspiration for the judgment	

philosopher	
	주장하다
any body of knowledge	
	~로 구성하다
an end and a means	

Paragraph E

	A를 B에 적용하다
in order to ~	
how to market effectively	
to what end	
two main attitudes toward ~	
the purposed of marketing	
	돈을 벌다
	전혀 무관한
the acquisition of ~	
	마케팅 전문 지식
as such	
	제안
neither of ~	
capture the significance of the end	
a field of knowledge	
a professional endeavor	
	~에 의해 정의되다
	따라서
deserve scrutiny	

Paragraph F

at this point	
becomes supremely relevant	
	아마도
all about means	
how to detect and prosecute	
	범죄자 활동
	그러므로
in an ethical sense	
ask A to B	
articulate the end or purpose	
	결국에
generalize to ~	

The safety and welfare of society	
the very same knowledge of means	
achieve a much less noble end	
such as personal profit	
via destructive, dangerous, reckless activity	
firefighting	
a seperate word	
arson	
	비슷하게도
	이용하다
the principles of marketing	
in an unprincipled way	
term for it	
	사기
the example of a doctor and a poisoner	
	똑같은 지식
divergent ends	
practice medicine	
	살인자

TEST

6

The risks agriculture faces in developing countries

VOCA

synthesis	통합

Paragraph A

distinguish A from B	A와 B를 구별하다
productive activities	생산적인 활동들
has a right to ~	~에 대한 권리를 가지고 있다
be hugely dependent on ~	~에 대단히 의존하다
two unique aspects	두 가지 독특한 측면들
make food production vulnerable	음식의 생산을 취약하게 만들다
at the same time	동시에
cultural values	문화적 가치들
be entrenched in ~	~에 자리 잡고 있다

Paragraph B

face major risks	주요한 위기에 직면하다
including extreme weather	극심한 날씨를 포함하여
long-term climate change	장기간의 기후 변화
price volatility	가격의 불안정
input and product markets	투입과 생산 시장
smallholder farmers	소작농들
in addition	덧붙여서
deal with	다루다
adverse environments	불리한 환경
both A and B	A와 B 둘 다
in terms of soil quality	토양의 질에 관해서
infrastructure	사회공공 기반시설
counter-intuitively	직감에 반하여, 이해하기 쉽지 않지만
prevalent	일반적인
in the developing world	후진국에서

Paragraph C

participants	참가자들
argue	주장하다
our biggest challenge	우리의 가장 큰 문제
address the underlying causes	기본적인 문제를 해결하다
inability to ensure sufficient food	충분한 음식 확보에 대한 무능력
identify as drivers of ~	~에 대한 원인으로서 인지하다
dependency on fossil fuels	화석연료의 의존성
unsupportive government policies	지지받지 못하는 정부 정책들

Paragraph D

mitigate the risk	위험을 완화하다
essayists	평론가들, 수필가들
call for	요청하다
state intervention	정부 개입
significantly reduce	상당히 줄이다
storage facilities	저장 시설들
reduce losses	손실을 줄이다
procurement	납품, 조달
stocks	재고품, 재고
mitigate wild swings in food prices	식품 가격에서의 지나친 변동을 완화하다
alleviate uncertainties about ~	~에 대한 불확실성을 완화시키다

Paragraph E

hold up	지지하다
social safety nets	사회 안전망
public welfare programmes	공공복지 프로그램들
address poverty	가난을 해결하다
reduce vulnerability to agriculture shocks	농업의 충격에 대한 취약성을 줄이다
commentators respond	시사 해설가는 답하다
cash transfers	현금 이체
necessarily translate into	반드시 옮기다(실행하다)
increased food security	증가된 식품 안정성
strengthen food production	식품 생산을 강화하다
raise incomes	소득을 올리다
regarding state subsidies	정부의 보조금에 대해
compensate for ~	~을 보상하다
the stranglehold exercised by ~	~에 의해 행해진 목조르기(압박)
beneficiary	수혜자, 수익자

not A, but B	A가 아니라 B이다
landowner	토지 소유자

Paragraph F

private insurance	개인 보험
commodity market	상품 시장
rural finance	농촌 금융
small-scale producers	작은 규모의 생산자들
allow for ~	~을 고려하다
investment in ~	~에 대한 투자
scheme	계획, 설계
encourage	장려하다, 권하다
the adoption of high-input agriculture practices	고강도 농업 실행의 채택
in the medium term	중기적으로
raise production costs	생산비를 올리다
beyond the value of their harvests	그들의 수확의 가치를 넘어
note	언급하다
become excessively financialised	과도하게 자금화되다, 과도하게 재정적으로 되다
contribute to ~	~에 기여하다
short-term price volatility	단기 가격 변동성
food insecurity	식품 불안정
participants	참가자들
emphasize	강조하다
transparency in markets	시장에서의 투명성
the impact of volatility	변동성(불안정)의 영향
make evident	명백히 하다
adequate stocks and supplies	적절한 재고와 공급
be available	이용 가능하다
contend	주장하다
agribusiness company	농업 관련 산업 회사
hold responsible for ~	~에 대한 책임이 있다
pay for negative side effects	부정적인 부작용에 대해 대가를 지불하다

Paragraph G

mention	언급하다
climate change	기후 변화
consequences for ~	~에 대한 결과
in addition to ~	~에 덧붙여서
crop yields	작물 수확량
magnitude	규모, 정도

the frequency of ~	~의 빈도
extreme weather events	극심한 기상 상태
small holder vulnerability	소작농의 취약성
the growing unpredictability of ~	~의 증가하는 예측 불가능성
weather-related risks	날씨와 관련된 위험들
according to ~	~에 따르면
solution	해법
develop crop varieties	작물 품종들을 개발하다
be resilient to ~	~에 대한 탄력이 있다
co-founder and executive director of ~	~에 대한 공동 설립자 그리고 전무이사
adopt policies	정책들을 채택하다
let peasants diversify	농부에게 다양하게 하다
species	종
varieties / breeds	품종들
make up	구성하다

Paragraph H

argue in favor of ~	~를 지지하다
community-based	공동체에 기반을 둔
autonomous risk management strategy	자율적 위험 관리 전략
collective action	공동의 행동
enhance	강화하다
synchronize	동시에 일어나다
with seasonal price conditions	계절적 가격 조건과 함께
strengthen	강화하다
bargaining power	교섭력
as a free good	무료로
organize	조직하다
in order to apply	적용하기 위해서
stakeholders	이해 당사자들, 주주들
work together	협력하다, 함께 일하다

Paragraph L

market share volatility	시장 점유율 불확실성
be worsen by ~	~에 의해 악화되다
the presence of ~	~의 존재
intermediary purchasers	중간 구매자들
take advantage of ~	~을 이용하다
vulnerability	취약성
dictate prices	가격을 좌우하다

gain greater control over ~	~에 대한 통제권을 갖다
minimise	최소화하다
founder and advisor to ~	~에 대한 설립자 그리고 고문
by subscription	신청에 의해
guarantee producers a fair price	생산자들에게 적정 가격을 보증하다
a risk-sharing model	위험공유 모델
distribution systems	분배 시스템
not only A, but also B	A뿐만 아니라 B도
give consumer more control over ~	소비자에게 ~에 대한 통제권을 주다

REVIEW

synthesis	통합

Paragraph A

	A와 B를 구별하다
	생산적인 활동들
	~에 대단히 의존하다
	~에 대한 권리를 가지고 있다
two unique aspects	
	음식의 생산을 취약하게 만들다
	동시에
	문화적 가치들
be entrenched in ~	

Paragraph B

	주요한 위기에 직면하다
	극심한 날씨를 포함하여
	장기간의 기후 변화
	가격의 불안정
	투입과 생산 시장
smallholder farmers	
	덧붙여서
	다루다
	불리한 환경
	A와 B 둘 다
	토양의 질에 관해서
	사회공공 기반시설
counter-intuitively	
	일반적인
	후진국에서

Paragraph C

	참가자들
	주장하다
	우리의 가장 큰 문제
	기본적인 문제를 해결하다
	충분한 음식 확보에 대한 무능력
identify as drivers of ~	

	화석연료의 의존성
	지지받지 못하는 정부 정책들

Paragraph D

	위험을 완화하다
essayists	
	요청하다
state intervention	
	상당히 줄이다
	저장 시설들
	손실을 줄이다
procurement	
stocks	
mitigate wild swings in food prices	
	~에 대한 불확실성을 완화시키다

Paragraph E

	지지하다
	사회 안전망
	공공복지 프로그램들
	가난을 해결하다
	농업의 충격에 대한 취약성을 줄이다
commentators respond	
	현금 이체
	반드시 옮기다(실행하다)
	증가된 식품 안정성
	식품 생산을 강화하다
	소득을 올리다
	정부의 보조금에 대해
	~을 보상하다
the stranglehold exercised by ~	
	수혜자, 수익자
not A, but B	
	토지 소유자

Paragraph F

	개인 보험
	상품 시장
	농촌 금융
	작은 규모의 생산자들

allow for ~	
	~에 대한 투자
	계획, 설계
	장려하다, 권하다
the adoption of high-input agriculture practices	
in the medium term	
	생산비를 올리다
	그들의 수확의 가치를 넘어
	언급하다
become excessively financialised	
	~에 기여하다
	단기 가격 변동성
	식품 불안정
	참가자들
	강조하다
	시장에서의 투명성
	변동성(불안정)의 영향
	명백히 하다
adequate stocks and supplies	
	이용 가능하다
	주장하다
agribusiness company	
	~에 대한 책임이 있다
	부정적인 부작용에 대해 대가를 지불하다

Paragraph G

	언급하다
	기후 변화
	~에 대한 결과
	~에 덧붙여서
	작물 수확량
	규모, 정도
the frequency of ~	~의 빈도
extreme weather events	
small holder vulnerability	
the growing unpredictability of ~	
	날씨와 관련된 위험들
	~에 따르면
	해법
	작물 품종들을 개발하다

	~에 대한 탄력이 있다
co-founder and executive director of ~	
adopt policies	
	농부에게 다양하게 하다
	종
	품종들
	구성하다

Paragraph H

	~를 지지하다
community-based	
autonomous risk management strategy	
	공동의 행동
	강화하다
	동시에 일어나다
with seasonal price conditions	
	강화하다
bargaining power	
as a free good	
	조직하다
	적용하기 위해서
stakeholders	
	협력하다, 같이 일하다

Paragraph L

market share volatility	
	~에 의해 악화되다
the presence of ~	
intermediary purchasers	
	~을 이용하다
	취약성
	가격을 좌우하다
	~에 대한 통제권을 갖다
minimise	최소화하다
founder and advisor to ~	
	신청에 의해
	생산자들에게 적정 가격을 보증하다
	위험공유 모델
distribution systems	

	A뿐만 아니라 B도
give consumer more control over ~	

PASSAGE 2
The Lost City

VOCA

an explorer's encounter with ~	탐험가의 ~와의 우연한 만남
the ruined city	멸망한 도시
the Inca civilization	잉카 문화

Paragraph A

be ready for ~	~을 준비하다
the greatest achievement of his life	그의 삶의 가장 위대한 성취
the remote hinterland	멀리 떨어진 오지
empire	제국
to locate the remains of city	도시의 유물을 찾기 위해서
lie on	놓여 있다
a high plateau	고원
at an elevation	높은 지대
descend	내려오다
a circuitous route	순환 경로
dramatic canyons	극적 협곡
mountain ranges	산맥

Paragraph B

set off	출발하다
have an advantage over ~	~에 대한 이점을 가지다
precede	선행하다, 앞서다
a track	오솔길
blast	폭파하다
enable A to B	A가 B 하는 것을 가능하게 하다
rubber	고무
be brought up by mules	노새에 의해 옮겨지다
previous travellers	이전의 여행객들
rejoin	재결합하다
thereby	그렇게 함으로써

substantial	상당한
pass through	거쳐 가다

Paragraph C

descent of the valley	계곡의 하강
arrange sufficient mules	충분한 노새를 준비하다
for the next stage of the trek	여행의 다음 단계를 위해서
companions	동료들
show no interest in accompanying	동행에 대해 관심을 보이지 않다
up the nearby hill	근처 언덕 위
ruins	유물들, 유적지
dull and damp	흐릿한 그리고 습한
keen on the prospect of climbing	등반에 대한 기대에 열정적인
relate	관련시키다
make the ascent	등반하다
without having the least expectation	최소의 기대도 가지지 않고

Paragraph D

approach	접근
in vivid style	생생한 스타일로
the ever-present possibility of ~	~에 대한 항상 존재하는 가능성
deadly snakes	치명적인 뱀들
capable of ~	~ 할 수 있는
make considerable springs	상당한 샘들(구멍들)을 만들다
in pursuit of their prey	그들의 먹이를 위해
a sense of mounting discovery	점차 증가하는 발견의 감각
come across	우연히 발견하다
great sweeps of terraces	큰 완만한 테라스
mausoleum	웅장한 무덤
, followed by ~	~로 이어지다
monumental staircases	기념비적인 계단들
ceremonial building	의식용 건물
unbelievable dream	믿을 수 없는 꿈
hold spellbound	황홀하게 하다

Paragraph E

a work of hindsight	뒤늦은 작품
journal entry	저널 항목
reveal	보여 주다
a much more gradual appreciation	더 많은 점진적 가치

achievement	성취
note down	적다
the dimension of ~	~에 대한 치수
at this stage	이 단계에서
the extent	범위
the importance of the site	그 유적지의 중요성
make use of ~	~을 이용하다

Paragraph F

soon after returning	돌아온 후 즉시
occur to ~	~에게 발생하다, 깨닫다
make a name for oneself	유명해지다
break the story to the world	그 이야기를 세상에 전하다
wonder whether ~	~인지 아닌지 궁금하다
the birthplace of ~	~의 발상지
chronicler	연대기 작가
the settlement	정착지
term	용어
refer to	말하다, 언급하다
flee from invaders	침입자로부터 도망가다
make desperate attempts to prove	증명하기 위해 필사적으로 시도하다
vision	시각
both A and B	A와 B 둘다
magnificent	훌륭한, 웅장한
inaccurate	정확하지 않은, 확실하지 않은
in the depth of the jungle	정글의 한가운데

Paragraph G

perplex	당혹하게 하다, 혼란시키다
archaeologist	고고학자
alike	똑같이
abandon	버리다
conquest	정복
references	자료들
existence so close to Cusco	Cusco에 아주 가까운 존재
in search of gold	금을 찾아서
gain wide acceptance	널리 받아들여지다
over the past few years	지난 수년에 걸쳐서
estate built by ~	~에 의해 세워진 재산
emperor	황제, 군주

escape the cold winters	추운 겨울들을 피하다
the elite	영향력 있는 사람들
monumental architecture	기념비적인 건축물
spectacular views	놀라운 광경
furthermore	더욱이
the particular architecture of ~	~에 대한 특별한 건축물
by custom	관습상
descendants	후손들

REVIEW

an explorer's encounter with ~	
	멸망한 도시
the Inca civilization	

Paragraph A

	~을 준비하다
	그의 삶의 가장 위대한 성취
the remote hinterland	
	제국
to locate the remains of city	
lie on	
	고원
	높은 지대
	내려오다
a circuitous route	
dramatic canyons	
mountain ranges	

Paragraph B

	출발하다
	~에 대한 이점을 가지다
	선행하다, 앞서다
	오솔길
blasted	
	A가 B 하는 것을 가능하게 하다
	고무
be brought up by mules	
	이전의 여행객들
	재결합하다
	그렇게 함으로써
	상당한
pass through	

Paragraph C

descent of the valley	
arrange sufficient mules	
for the next stage of the trek	

	동료들
show no interest in accompanying	
up the nearby hill	
	유물들, 유적지
	흐릿한 그리고 습한
keen on the prospect of climbing	
	관련시키다
	등반하다
without having the least expectation	

Paragraph D

approach	
in vivid style	
the ever-present possibility of ~	
deadly snakes	
	~ 할 수 있는
make considerable springs	
in pursuit of their prey	
a sense of mounting discovery	
	우연히 발견하다
great sweeps of terraces	
mausoleum	
	~로 이어지다
monumental staircases	
ceremonial building	
unbelievable dream	
	황홀하게 하다

Paragraph E

a work of hindsight	
journal entry	
	보여 주다
a much more gradual appreciation	
	성취
	적다
	~에 대한 치수
	이 단계에서
the extent	

the importance of the site	
	~을 이용하다

Paragraph F

soon after returning	
occur to ~	
make a name for oneself	
break the story to the world	
wonder whether ~	
the birthplace of ~	
chronicler	
	용어
	말하다, 언급하다
	정착지
	침입자로부터 도망가다
make desperate attempts to prove	
	시각
	A와 B 둘 다
	훌륭한, 웅장한
	정확하지 않은, 확실하지 않은
in the depth of the jungle	

Paragraph G

	당혹하게 하다, 혼란시키다
	고고학자
alike	
	버리다
	정복
	자료들
existence so close to Cusco	
	금을 찾아서
	널리 받아들여지다
	지난 수년에 걸쳐서
estate built by ~	
emperor	
	추운 겨울들을 피하다
	영향력 있는 사람들
monumental architecture	
	놀라운 광경
	더욱이

the particular architecture of ~	
	관습상
	후손들

The Benefits of Being Bilingual

VOCA

bilingual	이중 언어의

Paragraph A

according to the latest figure	최근의 수치에 따르면
the majority of ~	대다수의 ~
bilingual / multilingual	이중 언어를 하는 / 다중 언어를 하는
have grown up	성장해 오고 있다
in the past	과거에는
be considered to ~	~로 간주되다
at a disadvantage	불리한 입장에
compared with monolingual peers	단일 언어를 하는 또래와 비교하면
over the past few decades	지난 수십 년에 걸쳐서
technological advances	기술적인 발전
allow A to B	A가 B 하는 것을 허락하다
look more deeply at	더 자세하게 관찰하다
interact with ~	~와 상호작용하다
the cognitive and neurological systems	인지적이고 신경학적인 시스템
thereby	그것에 의해
identify	확인하다, 인지하다

Paragraph B

active	활동적인
at the same time	동시에
all at once	동시에
in sequential order	순차적으로
long before	훨씬 전에
activate	활성화하다
as well	또한
at least	적어도
during the earlier stages of ~	~의 이른 단계 동안
word recognition	단어 인지
activation	활성화

auditory input	청각 입력
corresponding words	상응하는 단어들
regardless of ~	~에 관계없이
belong to ~	~에 속하다
the most compelling evidence	가장 강력한 증거
phenomenon	현상
eye movements	눈의 움직임들
a set of objects	일련의 물건들
look at ~	~을 보다
sound like ~	~처럼 들리다
In case like this	이와 같은 경우에
language co-activation	언어 공동 활성화
occur	발생하다, 일어나다
map onto words	단어들을 연관시키다

Paragraph C

deal with	다루다
persistent linguistic competition	지속적인 언어적 경쟁
result in difficulties	어려움들을 야기하다(초래하다)
cause A to B	A 가 B를 초래하다
tip-of-the tongue states	혀끝 상태, 입안에서 맴돌다
bring a word to mind	단어를 떠오르게 하다
as a result	그 결과로써
the constant juggling of ~	~에 대한 지속적인 저글링
access	접근하다
at any given time	주어진 시간에
preform better on tasks	일에 있어 더 잘 수행하다
name	지명하다, 명명하다
the word's font	단어의 글꼴
excel at task	일에 있어 뛰어나다
tap into the ability	능력을 이용하다
ignore	무시하다
perceptual information	인지에 대한 정보
focus on the relevant aspects	관련 측면에 집중하다
be better at ~	~를 잘하다
switch A from B	A에서 B로 바꾸다
categorize	분류하다
by shape	형태로
reflect	반영하다, 보여 주다
cognitive control	인지 통제
rapid changes of strategy	전략에 대한 급격한 변화

Paragraph D

neurological roots of ~	~에 대한 신경학상의 근원
extend to ~	~까지 연장하다
associated with ~	~와 관련해서
sensory processing	감각 과정
adolescents	청소년들
without intervening background noise	주변 소음의 개입 없이
brain stem responses	뇌 줄기 반응
in the presence of ~	~의 면전에서
considerably	상당히, 현저히
encode	부호화하다
fundamental frequency	기본적인 주파수(진동수)
related to pitch perception	음색 지각과 관련된

Paragraph E

cognitive and sensory processing	인지와 감각처리
bilingual adults	이중 언어 성인들
acquire a third language	제2의 언어를 습득하다
be rooted in ~	~에 근원을 두다
reduce interference	방해를 줄이다

Paragraph F

indicate	보여 주다
keep the cognitive mechanisms sharp	인지 체계의 뚜렷함을 유지하다
recruit alternate brain networks	교류하는 뇌 구조를 구성하다
compensate for ~	~을 보상하다
become damaged	손상되다
during aging	나이가 드는 동안
relative to ~	~에 비하여
lead to	야기하다 초래하다
real-world health benefits	현실 세계의 건강상 이점들
a degenerative brain disease	퇴행성의 뇌 질병
initial symptom of the disease	그 질병의 초기 증상
in a follow-up study	다음의 연구에서
compare	비교하다
on the severity of ~	~에 대한 심각성
surprisingly	놀랍게도
counterpart	상대방
outward behaviour	표면상의 행동
go farther	더 나아가다

Paragraph G

Furthermore	더욱이
a tinkling sound	딸랑딸랑 소리
puppet	인형
halfway	중간에
in order to get a reward	보상을 받기 위해서
infant	유아
adjust	적응하다
B as well as A	A뿐만 아니라 B도
navigate	잘 다루다
impart advantages	장점들을 주다
transfer far beyond language	언어의 범위 이상을 전달하다

REVIEW

	이중 언어의

Paragraph A

	최근의 수치에 따르면
	대다수의 ~
	이중 언어를 하는 / 다중 언어를 하는
	성장해 오고 있다
	과거에는
	~로 간주되다
at a disadvantage	
compared with monolingual peers	
	지난 수십 년에 걸쳐서
	기술적인 발전
	A가 B 하는 것을 허락하다
	더 자세하게 관찰하다
	~와 상호작용하다
the cognitive and neurological systems	
	그것에 의해
	확인하다, 인지하다

Paragraph B

	활동적인
	동시에
all at once	
in sequential order	
	훨씬 전에
	활성화하다
	또한
	적어도
	~의 이른 단계 동안
	단어 인지
	활성화
auditory input	
corresponding words	
	~에 관계없이
	~에 속하다
	가장 강력한 증거

	현상
	눈의 움직임들
a set of objects	
	~을 보다
	~처럼 들리다
In case like this	
language co-activation	
	발생하다, 일어나다
map onto words	

Paragraph C

	다루다
	지속적인 언어적 경쟁
	어려움들을 야기하다(초래하다)
	A가 B를 초래하다
tip-of-the-tongue states	
bring a word to mind	
	그 결과로써
the constant juggling of	
	접근하다
	주어진 시간에
	일에 있어 더 잘 수행하다
	지명하다, 명명하다
the word's font	
	일에 있어 뛰어나다
	능력을 이용하다
	무시하다
perceptual information	
focus on the relevant aspects	
	~를 잘하다
switch A from B	
categorize	
	형태로
	반영하다, 보여 주다
cognitive control	인지 통제
	전략에 대한 급격한 변화

Paragraph D

neurological roots of ~	
	~까지 연장하다
	~와 관련해서
sensory processing	
	청소년들
	주변 소음의 개입 없이
	뇌 줄기 반응
	~의 면전에서
	상당히, 현저히
encode	
fundamental frequency	
related to pitch perception	

Paragraph E

cognitive and sensory processing	
	이중 언어 성인들
	제2의 언어를 습득하다
be rooted in ~	~에 근원을 두다
	방해를 줄이다

Paragraph F

	보여 주다
keep the cognitive mechanisms sharp	
recruit alternate brain networks	
	보상하다
become damaged	
	나이가 드는 동안
	~에 비하여
	야기하다, 초래하다
real-world health benefits	
	퇴행성의 뇌 질병
	그 질병의 초기 증상
in a follow-up study	
	비교하다
on the severity of ~	
	놀랍게도
	상대방

outward behaviour	
go farther	

Paragraph G

	더욱이
a tinkling sound	
puppet	
	중간에
	보상을 받기 위해서
	유아
	적응하다
	A뿐만 아니라 B도
	잘 다루다
impart advantages	
	언어의 범위 이상을 전달하다

TEST
7

Flying tortoises

VOCA

an airborne reintroduction programme	공수(비행) 재도입 프로그램
conservationists	자연 보호론자들
take significant steps	중요한 조치들을 취하다
the endangered tortoise	멸종 위기에 처한 거북이(육지거북이)

Paragraph A

spiny cacti	가시가 있는 선인장류
uneven lava plains	고르지 못한 용암 평원들
separate A from B	A를 B와 분리하다(나누다)
the interior of ~	~의 내부
the Pacific Ocean	태평양
distinct volcanoes	독특한 화산들
resemble	닮다, 유사하다
a lunar landscape	달 풍경
the thick vegetation	빽빽한 초목
at the skirt of ~	~의 가장자리에
respite from ~	~로부터의 일시적 중단(휴식)
the barren terrain	불모의 지역
the inhospitable environment	삶이나 성장에 좋지 않은 환경
A be home to B	A는 B의 서식지이다
birth	태생, 출생
be colonized by ~	~에 의해 식민지가 되다
mainland	본토, 대륙
ancestral	조상의
settle on the individual islands	각각의 섬에 정착하다
the different populations	다른 개체군들
adapt to ~	~에 적응하다
give rise to	일으키다, 초래하다
at least	적어도
subspecies	아종
agree with ~	~의 성미에 맞다(잘 맞다)
in the absence of ~	~의 부재로

significant predators	상당한 약탈자들
grow to become ~	성장하여 ~가 되다
on the planet	지구상에서
weigh	무게가 나가다
exceed in length	길이에 있어 초과하다
for more than a century	100년 이상 동안

Paragraph B

human arrival	인류의 도착
number	총계가 ~이 되다
from the 17th century onwards	17세기부터
pirate	해적
take a few on board	몇 개를 선적하다
whaling ships	고래잡이배들
exploitation	약탈, 탈취
exponentially	기하급수적으로
relatively immobile	상대적으로 움직일 수 없는
capable of surviving	생존할 수 있는
be taken on board	선적되다
food supplies	음식 공급
during long ocean passages	오랜 항해 동안
be processed into ~	~로 가공되다(처리되다)
in total	전체적으로
estimated	추정된
be exacerbated	악화되다
settlers	정착민들
habitat	서식지
clear land for agriculture	농업을 위해 개간하다
alien species	외래종
range from A to B	범위가 A부터 B에 달하다
prey on the eggs	알을 잡아먹다
damage or destroy	손상시키고 파괴시키다

Paragraph C

original subspecies	원래의 아종
be highly endangered	매우 멸종 위기에 처하다
a tortoise-breeding centre	거북 번식 센터
dedicated to protecting	보호하는 데 전념하는
be extremely successful	아주 성공적이다
deal with an overpopulation problem	과잉 인구의 문제를 다루다

Paragraph D

pressing	긴급한
captive-bred	포획 번식한, 인공적으로 번식한
be reintroduced into the wild	야생으로 다시 소개되다
hardened shells	딱딱한 조개(껍데기)
be sufficient to ~	~에 충분하다
protect A from B	A를 B로부터 보호하다
become too large to transport	너무나 커서 이송하기 힘들게 되다

Paragraph E

repatriation efforts	송환 노력
be carried out	수행되다
carried on the backs of ~	~의 등에 업혀
treacherous hikes	위험한 도보
along narrow trails	좁은 길을 따라
liaison officer	연락 장교
gather	모이다
work out more ambitious reintroduction	더 야망 있는 재도입을 수행하다
aim	목적, 목표
move A to B	A를 B로 옮기다
locations close to A	A에 가까운 지역들

Paragraph F

unprecedented effort	전례 없는 노력
provide A with B	A에게 B를 제공하다
B as well as A	A뿐만 아니라 B도
the logistical support of ~	~에 대한 수송의 지원
captain and crew	선장과 선원
a rear double door	후면 이중문
be suited for cargo	화물에 적합하다
a custom crate	주문 상자
be designed to hold up	수용하도록 만들어지다
approach the maximum payload	극도의 탑재량에 다다르다
on the edge of the capabilities	수용 한계에
around the clock	24시간 내내
transport	수송
meanwhile	반면에
park wardens	공원 관리인들
drop off ahead of time	시간 전에 내리다
clear landing sites	착륙 지점을 치우다
thick brush, cacti and lava rocks	두꺼운 관목, 선인장류 그리고 용암암

Paragraph G

upon release	방출될 때
juvenile tortoise	어린 거북이
spread out	퍼지다
ancestral territory	조상의 영토
investigate new surroundings	새로운 환경을 살피다
feed on the vegetation	식물을 먹고 살다
come across	우연히 마주치다
a fully grown giant	완전히 자란 거대한 동물
lumber around	주변을 돌아다니다
side by side	나란히
the regeneration of an ancient species	오랜 종들의 재건

REVIEW

an airborne reintroduction programme	공수(비행)의 재도입 프로그램
	자연보호론자들
	중요한 조치들을 취하다
	멸종 위기에 처한 거북이

Paragraph A

spiny cacti	
uneven lava plains	
	A를 B와 분리하다(나누다)
the interior of ~	~의 내부
	태평양
	독특한 화산들
	닮다, 유사하다
a lunar landscape	
the thick vegetation	
	~의 가장자리에
	~로부터의 일시적 중단(휴식)
the barren terrain	
	삶이나 성장에 좋지 않은 환경
A be home to B	
birth	
	~에 의해 식민지가 되다
	본토, 대륙
	조상의
	각각의 섬에 정착하다
	다른 개체군들
	~에 적응하다
give rise to	
	적어도
	아종
agree with ~	
	~의 부재로
	상당한 약탈자들
grow to become ~	
	지구상에서
	무게가 나가다
	길이에 있어 초과하다
for more than a century	

Paragraph B

	인류의 도착
	총계가 ~이 되다
from the 17th century onwards	17세기부터
pirate	
take a few on board	
whaling ships	
	약탈
	기하급수적으로
	상대적으로 움직일 수 없는
	생존할 수 있는
be taken on board	
food supplies	음식 공급
during long ocean passages	
be processed into ~	
	전체적으로
estimated	
	악화되다
	정착민들
	서식지
clear land for agriculture	
alien species	
	범위가 A부터 B에 달하다
	알을 잡아먹다

Paragraph C

original subspecies	
	매우 멸종 위기에 처하다
a tortoise-breeding centre	
	보호하는 데 전념하다
	아주 성공적이다
	과잉 인구의 문제를 다루다
	손상시키고 파괴시키다

Paragraph D

	긴급한
captive-bred	
	야생으로 다시 소개되다
hardened shells	

	~에 충분하다
	A를 B로부터 보호하다
become too large to transport	

Paragraph E

repatriation efforts	
	수행되다
carried on the backs of ~	
	위험한 도보
along narrow trails	좁은 길을 따라
	연락 장교
	모이다
work out more ambitious reintroduction	
	목적, 목표
	A를 B로 옮기다
	A에 가까운 지역들

Paragraph F

	전례 없는 노력
	A에게 B를 제공하다
	A뿐만 아니라 B도
the logistical support of ~	
	선장과 선원
a rear double door	
	화물에 적합하다
a custom crate	
be designed to hold up	
approach the maximum payload	
on the edge of the capabilities	
	24시간 내내
	반면에
	공원 관리인들
	시간 전에 내리다
clear landing sites	
thick brush, cacti and lava rocks	

Paragraph G

upon release	
	어린 거북이
	퍼지다
ancestral territory	
	새로운 환경을 살피다
	식물을 먹고 살다
	우연히 마주치다
a fully grown giant	
lumber around	
	나란히
the regeneration of an ancient species	

PASSAGE 2
The intersection of Health Sciences and Geography

VOCA

Paragraph A

eradicate	근절하다
due to improvements	발전 때문에
vaccinations	백신 접종
the availability of healthcare	건강 관리의 유용성
be more prevalent	널리 퍼져 있다
be far more globalised	훨씬 더 세계화되다
than ever before	전보다 더
come into contact with ~	~와 연락하게 되다
live closer to ~	~에 가까이 살다
as a result	그 결과로써
super-viruses	슈퍼 바이러스
infections resistant to antibiotics	항생제에 저항력이 있는 감염
become common	일반화되다

Paragraph B

geography	지리학
play a very large role in ~	~에 있어 중대한 역할을 하다
the health concerns	건강 염려
depend on ~	~에 좌우하다
in a different geographical region	다른 지질학적인 지역에서
malaria-prone areas	말라리아에 걸리기 쉬운 지역들
tropical regions	열대 지역들
foster	육성하다, 만들다
a damp environment	습한 환경
mosquitos	모기들
much less	훨씬 덜
in high-altitude deserts	높은 고도의 사막들

Paragraph C

geographical factors	지질학적인 요인들
well-being	건강
in a very obvious way	분명한 방법에 있어
the massive amounts of ~	~에 대한 거대한 양
asthma / lung problems	천식(폐) 문제들
the massive number of cars	엄청난 차량의 수
in addition to factories	공장에 덧붙여서
ran on coal power	석탄의 동력에 작동하다
rapid industrialization	급격한 산업화
lead to	야기하다, 초래하다
the cutting down of forests	숲의 축소
the expansion of ~	~의 확대
fight the pollution	오염에 맞서 싸우다

Paragraph D

the field of health geography	건강지리학 분야
come into	나오다, 일어나다
polio	소아마비
re-emerging	다시 나타나는
respiratory diseases	호흡기 질환들
continue to spread	계속해서 확산되다
fight to find	찾기 위해 싸우다(분투하다)
the combination of knowledge	지식의 결합
on the other hand	다른 한편으로는
regarding ~	~에 대한
analyse and interpret	분석하고 해석하다
geographical information	지리학적인 정보
the aim of this hybrid science	혼성 과학의 목적
create solutions	해결책을 만들다
geography-based health problems	지질학에 기반을 둔 건강 문제들
be prone to illness	병에 걸리기 쉽다
lead to	야기하다
the eradication of ~	~의 근절
the prevention of ~	~의 예방
treat illness and disease	질병과 질환을 치료하다
specific to ~	~에 특별한(특정한)

Paragraph E

the frequency	빈도
overlay the data	자료를 덧붙이다
see if ~	~인지 여부를 확인하다
a correlation between ~	~ 사이의 상호관계
health geographers	보건 지리학자들
be more likely to be taken ill	더 병에 걸릴 것 같다
as compared with ~	~와 비교해서
as health workers	의료 종사자로서
epidemiology	역학, 의생태학
relate to ~	~와 연관되다

Paragraph F

the interactions between ~	~ 사이의 상호작용
lead to illness	질병을 야기하다
in places	장소들에서
high levels of pollution	높은 단계의 오염
categorize A into B	A를 B로 분류하다
local and global scales	지역적이고 세계적인 규모
map	지도로 나타내다
attempt to identify the reasons	이유를 확인하는 것을 시도하다
behind an increase or decrease in ~	~에 있어 증가와 감소 이면에
halt the further spread	더 많은 확산을 막다
re-emergence of ~	~의 재출현
in vulnerable populations	취약한 인구에 있어서

Paragraph G

subcategory	하위 범주
healthcare provision	건강 지원
the availability of healthcare resources	건강 자원에 대한 유용성
lack thereof	그것에 대한(유용성에 대한) 부족
a large discrepancy between ~	~ 사이의 큰 차이
in different socal classes	다른 사회적 계층들에서
income brackets	소득층들
attempt to ~	~을 시도하다
assess the levels of healthcare	건강 관리 수준을 평가하다
get medical attention	치료를 받다
be on the frontline of ~	~의 최전선에 있다
make recommendations	추천하다
regarding policy	정책과 관련하여

Paragraph H

overlook	간과하다
constitute	구성하다
no matter where	어디에서든
keep people safe and well	사람을 안전하고 건강하게 지키다

REVIEW

Paragraph A

	근절하다
	발전 때문에
vaccinations	
	건강 관리의 유용성
	널리 퍼져 있다
	훨씬 더 세계화되다
	전보다 더
come into contact with	
	~에 더 가까이 살다
	그 결과로써
super-viruses	
infections resistant to antibiotics	
	일반화되다

Paragraph B

	지리학
	~에 있어 중대한 역할을 하다
	건강 염려
	~에 좌우하다
in a different geographical region	
malaria-prone areas	
	열대 지역들
	육성하다, 만들다
	습한 환경
	모기들
	훨씬 덜
in high-altitude deserts	

Paragraph C

geographical factors	
	건강
in a very obvious way	
the massive amounts of ~	
	천식(폐) 문제들
	엄청난 차량의 수

	공장에 덧붙여서
ran on coal power	
	급격한 산업화
	야기하다, 초래하다
	숲의 축소
	~의 확대
	오염에 맞서 싸우다

Paragraph D

the field of health geography	
	나오다, 일어나다
polio	
	다시 나타나는
	호흡기 질환들
continue to spread	
fight to find	
the combination of knowledge	
	다른 한편으로는
regarding ~	
	분석하고 해석하다
	지리학적인 정보
the aim of this hybrid science	
	해결책을 만들다
geography-based health problems	
	병에 걸리기 쉽다
	야기하다
	~의 근절
	~의 예방
	질병과 질환을 치료하다
specific to ~	

Paragraph E

	빈도
overlay the data	
see if ~	
	~ 사이의 상호관계
health geographers	
be more likely to be taken ill	
	~와 비교해서
	의료 종사자로서
epidemiology	
relate to ~	

Paragraph F

the interactions between ~	
	질병을 야기하다
	장소들에서
high levels of pollution	
	A를 B로 분류하다
local and global scales	
	지도로 나타내다
attempt to identify the reasons behind an increase or decrease in ~	
	더 많은 확산을 막다
re-emergence of ~	
	취약한 인구에 있어서

Paragraph G

subcategory	
	건강 지원
the availability of healthcare resources	
lack thereof	
a large discrepancy between ~	
in different socal classes	
	소득층들
	~을 시도하다
assess the levels of healthcare	
	치료를 받다
be on the frontline of ~	
	추천하다
	정책과 관련하여

Paragraph H

	간과하다
	구성하다
no matter where	
	사람을 안전하고 건강하게 지키다

PASSAGE 3
Music and the emotions

VOCA

neuroscientist	신경과학자

Paragraph 1

make us feel	우리를 느끼게 하다
on the one hand	한편으로는
purely abstract art form	순전히 추상적인 예술 형태
devoid of language	언어가 없는
explicit ideas	분명한 아이디어들
and yet	그런데도
manage to touch us deeply	우리를 깊이 감동시키다
betray the symptoms of emotional arousal	감정적인 흥분 증상을 드러내다
pupils	동공들
dilate	팽창하다
pulse and blood pressure	맥박과 혈압
the electrical conductance of ~	~의 전기 전도성
cerebellum	소뇌, 작은 골
associated with ~	~과 연관된
become strangely active	기이하게도 활동적이 되다
re-directed to ~	~로 방향이 바뀐
in other words	다시 말해서
stir	자극하다
at our biological roots	생물학적인 근원에서

Paragraph 2

a recent paper	최근 논문
mark an important step	중요한 단계를 기록하다
reveal	보여 주다
the precise underpinnings of ~	~에 대한 정확한 기반
the potent pleasurable stimulus	강력한 즐거움의 자극
involve	포함하다
plenty of fancy technology	많은 멋진 기술
including ~	~와 같은, ~을 포함하는

the experiment itself	실험 그 자체
rather straightforward	오히려 간단한
screen	선별하다, 가리다
respond to ~	~에 반응하다
chills	냉담함
advertisements requesting ~	~을 요청하는 광고
instrumental music	기악곡
narrow down the subject pool to ten	피실험자 인원을 10명으로 줄이다
bring in ~	~을 소개하다
virtually	사실상
be represented	보여지다
be monitored	조사되다
combine methodology	기술들(방법론들)을 결합하다
obtain	얻다, 획득하다
an impressively exact and detailed portrait	놀랄 정도로 정확하고 세부적인 묘사
trigger	야기하다, 초래하다
the production of dopamine	도파민 생산
a key role in setting people's moods	사람의 감정을 정하는 데 중요한 역할
neurons	신경 단위들
the dorsal and ventral regions	등과 배 부분들
be linked with ~	~와 연결되어 있다
this finding	이 결과

Paragraph 3

significant	중요한
the finding	결과
caudate	꼬리형의
involved in learning	배우는 데 관련된
stimulus-response associations	자극 반응 관련성
anticipate	기대하다, 예상하다
reward stimuli	보상 자극
participants	참여자들
anticipatory phase	예상하는 단계
predict the arrival of ~	~의 등장을 예견하다
what A be up to	A가 무엇을 하는지
acoustic climax	음향의 최고조
after all	결국
typically	일반적으로, 전형적으로
associate A with B	A를 B와 연관시키다
surges of dopamine	도파민의 증가

this cluster of cells	세포들의 무리
the melodic pattern	음악적인 구조
unresolved	미정의(uncertain)

Paragraph 4

look at	조사하다
at least to the outsider	적어도 외부인들에게
a labyrinth of intricate patterns	복잡한 구조의 미로
turn out	판명되다
symphony	교향악
break down	무너지다, 고장나다
become unpredictable	예측 불가능하게 되다
annoyingly boring	화가 날 정도로 지루한
demonstrate	보여 주다
adapt to ~	~에 적응하다
predictable rewards	예상될 수 있는 대가(보상)
get excited	흥분하다
a key note	중요한 음
in the beginning of ~	~의 초반에
most of the rest of the piece	대부분의 곡의 나머지
in the studious avoidance of ~	~의 애써 피함에 있어서
at the end	마지막에
the longer A, the greater B	A가 길면 길수록 B는 더더욱 크다
emotional release	감정적 표출

Paragraph 5

psychological principle	심리학적인 원리
musicologist	음악학자
analyse	분석하다
be defined by its flirtation with ~	~에 사로잡힘에 의해 정의된다
submission to ~	~에 굴복
our expectations of order	순서에 대한 우리의 기대
dissect 50 measures of the masterpiece	명작의 50박자들을 분석(해부)하다
begin with the clear statement	명료한 표현으로 시작하다
a rhythmic and harmonic pattern	리듬감 있고 조화로운 형식
in an ingenious tonal dance	독창적인 음색의 춤
hold off repeating it	그것의 반복을 미루다(막다)
instead	대신에
variation	변형, 변화
preserve an element of uncertainty	불확실의 요소들을 유지하다
beg for one chord	한 가지 코드를 간청하다

Paragraph 6

according to ~	~에 따르면
the suspenseful tension	박진감 있는 긴장
arise	발생하다, 생기다
unfulfilled expectations	실현되지 않은 기대
focus on ~	~에 집중하다
refer to ~	~을 언급하다(말하다)
the real world of images and experiences	이미지와 경험들의 실제 세계
connotative meaning	함축적인 의미
come from ~	~의 결과이다
the unfolding events	전개되는 일, 전개 과정
embodied meaning	구체화된 의미
invoke and then ignore	호소하고 그리고 무시하다
uncertainty	불확실성
triggers the surge of dopamine	도파민의 증가를 야기하다
struggle to figure out	알아내려 노력하다
predict some of the notes	몇 가지 음들을 예견하다
keep listening	계속해서 듣다
wait expectantly for our reward	기대하여 우리의 보상을 기다리다

REVIEW

neuroscientist	

Paragraph 1

	우리를 느끼게 하다
	한편으로는
purely abstract art form	
devoid of language	
	분명한 아이디어들
and yet	
manage to touch us deeply	
betray the symptoms of emotional arousal	
pupils	
dilate	
pulse and blood pressure	
the electrical conductance of ~	
cerebellum	
	~과 연관된
become strangely active	
re-directed to ~	
	다시 말해서
	자극하다
at our biological roots	

Paragraph 2

a recent paper	
mark an important step	
	보여 주다
the precise underpinnings of ~	
the potent pleasurable stimulus	
	포함하다
plenty of fancy technology	
	~와 같은, ~을 포함하는
the experiment itself	
rather straightforward	
	선별하다, 가리다
respond to ~	
chills	

advertisements requesting ~	
	기악곡
narrow down the subject pool to ten	
bring in ~	
	사실상
be represented	
be monitored	
combine methodology	
	얻다, 획득하다
an impressively exact and detailed portrait	
	야기하다, 초래하다
the production of dopamine	
a key role in setting people's moods	
neurons	
the dorsal and ventral regions	
	~와 연결되어 있다
this finding	

Paragraph 3

	중요한
	결과
in the caudate	
involved in learning	
stimulus-response associations	
	기대하다, 예상하다
reward stimuli	
	참여자들
anticipatory phase	
predict the arrival of ~	
what A be up to	
acoustic climax	
	결국
	일반적으로, 전형적으로
associate A with B	
surges of dopamine	
this cluster of cells	
the melodic pattern	
	미정의(uncertain)

Paragraph 4

	조사하다
at least to the outsider	
a labyrinth of intricate patterns	
	판명되다
symphony	
	무너지다, 고장 나다
	예측 불가능하게 되다
annoyingly boring	
	보여 주다
	~에 적응하다
	예상될 수 있는 대가(보상)
	흥분하다
	중요한 음
	~의 초반에
most of the rest of the piece	
in the studious avoidance of ~	
	마지막에
	A가 길면 길수록 B는 더더욱 크다
emotional release	

Paragraph 5

psychological principle	
musicologist	
	분석하다
be defined by its flirtation with ~	
submission to ~	
our expectations of order	
dissect 50 measures of the masterpiece	
begin with the clear statement	
a rhythmic and harmonic pattern	
in an ingenious tonal dance	
hold off repeating it	
	대신에
	변형, 변화
preserve an element of uncertainty	
beg for one chord	

Paragraph 6

	~에 따르면
the suspenseful tension	
	발생하다, 생기다
unfulfilled expectations	
	~에 집중하다
	~을 언급하다(말하다)
the real world of images and experiences	
connotative meaning	
come from ~	
the unfolding events	
embodied meaning	
invoke and then ignore	
	불확실성
triggers the surge of dopamine	
struggle to figure out	
predict some of the notes	
	계속해서 듣다
wait expectantly for our reward	

TEST

8

The History of Glass

VOCA

Paragraph 1

from our earliest origins	기원 초기부터
make use of ~	~을 이용하다(사용하다)
historians	역사학자들
form	형성되다, 형성시키다
the mouth of a volcano	화산의 입구
as a result of the intense heat	강력한 열의 결과로서
an eruption	분출
melt	녹이다
spear	창
archaeologist	고고학자
evidence	증거
man-made glass	사람이 만든 유리
date back to ~	~까지 거슬러 올라가다
take the form of ~	~의 형태를 취하다
glaze	광택제
coat stone beads	돌구슬을 칠하다
hollow glass container	속이 빈 용기
a layer of molten glass	용해된 유리의 층

Paragraph 2

glass blowing	유리 불기
the most common way	가장 일반적인 방법
due to impurities	불순물 때문에
raw material	원료
be tinted by	~에 의해 착색되다
the addition of materials	물질의 첨가
guard	보호하다
required to ~	~ 하기 위해 요구된
very closely	매우 극비리에
it was not until ~	~까지는 아니었다

empire collapse	제국이 무너지다
become widespread	널리 퍼지게 되다
onwards	계속, 앞으로
gain a reputation for ~	~로 명성을 얻다
craftsmen	장인들
set up glassworks	유리 공장을 설립하다

Paragraph 3

a major milestone	획기적인 이정표
with the invention of ~	~의 발명과 함께
glass manufacturer	유리 제조업자
attempt to counter	(악 영향에) 대응을 시도하다
the effect of clouding	흐림 효과
introduce lead to ~	~에 납을 도입하다
decorate	장식하다
a higher refractive index	높은 굴절률
add to brilliance and beauty	화려함과 아름다움을 더하다
invaluable to the optical industry	광학 산업에 매우 귀중한
thanks to ~	~ 덕택에
optical lenses	광학 렌즈, 시각 렌즈
astronomical telescopes, microscopes	천문 망원경, 현미경
and the like	기타 등등
become possible	가능하게 되다

Paragraph 4

the repeal of Act	법령의 폐지
be placed on the amount of glass	많은 양의 유리에 부과되다
be levied continuously	계속해서 부과되다
revolutionary building	혁신적인 건물
encourage	촉진하다
in public, domestic and horticultural architecture	공공에서, 가정의, 원예 건축
with the advancement of science	과학의 진보와 함께
the development of better technology	더 나은 기술의 발전

Paragraph 5

capable of producing	생산 능력 있는
quicker than any previous production method	다른 이전 생산 방법보다 더 빠른
automated machine	자동화된 기계
founder	설립자

be installed	설치되다
impressive	놀라운
become cut off from ~	~로부터 차단되다
glass suppliers	유리 공급업자들
become part of the scientific sector	과학 부분의 일부분이 되다
previous to this	이것에 앞서
as a craft	공예품으로서
rather than a precious science	정밀한 과학보다는

Paragraph 6

hi-tech industry	첨단 기술 산업
in a fiercely competitive global market	치열하게 경쟁적인 세계 시장에서
be critical to ~	~에게 중요하다
be capable of ~	~ 할 능력이 있다
feature	특징을 가지다
in every aspect of our lives	우리 삶의 모든 측면에서
beverages	음료들
numerous foodstuffs	수많은 식품들
B as well as A	A뿐만 아니라 B도
medicines and cosmetics	의약품과 화장품들

Paragraph 7

be ideal for ~	~에 이상적이다
growing consumer concern	증가하는 소비자의 염려
green issues	환경 문제들
used glass	중고 유리
be sent to landfill	매립지로 보내지다
be melt down	녹여지다
fuel and production costs	연료와 생산 비용
the need for raw materials	원자재의 필요성
be quarried	캐내지다
save precious resources	귀중한 자원을 절약하다

REVIEW

Paragraph 1

from our earliest origins	기원 초기부터
	~을 이용하다(사용하다)
	역사학자들
form	
the mouth of a volcano	
	강력한 열의 결과로서
	분출
	녹이다
	창
	고고학자
	증거
	사람이 만든 유리
	~까지 거슬러 올라가다
take the form of ~	
	광택제
coat stone beads	
hollow glass container	
a layer of molten glass	

Paragraph 2

glass blowing	
the most common way	
	불순물 때문에
	원료
be tinted by	
the addition of materials	
	보호하다
required to ~	
very closely	
it was not until ~	
empire collapse	
	널리 퍼지게 되다
onwards	
	~로 명성을 얻다
	장인들
	유리 공장을 설립하다

Paragraph 3

a major milestone	
	~의 발명과 함께
	유리 제조업자
attempt to counter	
the effect of clouding	
introduce lead to	
	장식하다
a higher refractive index	
add to brilliance and beauty	
invaluable to the optical industry	
	~ 덕택에
optical lenses	
astronomical telescopes, microscopes	
and the like	
	가능하게 되다

Paragraph 4

the repeal of Act	
be placed on the amount of glass	
be levied continuously	
	혁신적인 건물
	촉진하다
in public, domestic and horticultural architecture	
with the advancement of science	
	더 나은 기술의 발전

Paragraph 5

capable of producing	
quicker than any previous production method	
	자동화된 기계
	설립자
	설치되다
impressive	
become cut off from ~	
glass suppliers	

become part of the scientific sector	
previous to this	
	공예품으로서
rather than a precious science	

Paragraph 6

	첨단 기술 산업
in a fiercely competitive global market	
	~에게 중요하다
	~ 할 능력이 있다
	특징을 가지다
in every aspect of our lives	
	음료들
numerous foodstuffs	
	A뿐만 아니라 B도
	의약품과 화장품들

Paragraph 7

	~에 이상적이다
growing consumer concern	
	환경 문제들
used glass	
be sent to landfill	
be melt down	
fuel and production costs	
the need for raw materials	
be quarried	
	귀중한 자원을 절약하다

PASSAGE 2
Bring back the big cats

VOCA

it is time to ~	~ 할 때이다
vanished native animals	사라진 토종 동물들

Paragraph 1

poem	시
describe hunting	사냥을 묘사하다
nothing seemed to fit	어느 것도 적합한 것이 없다
an animal bone	동물 뼈
date from ~	~부터 시작되다
lynx	스라소니
a large spotted cat	큰 얼룩이 진 고양이
tasselled ears	술이 달린 귀(귀 뒤에 뾰족한 털)
presume	가정하다
die out	멸종하다
inhabitants	거주민들
take up farming	농사를 시작하다
compelling evidence	설득력 있는 증거
one and the same animal	동일한 동물
bring forward	제시하다
estimated extinction date	예상된 멸종 시기
by roughly 5,000 years	약 5,000년 차이

Paragraph 2

the last glimpse	마지막 접촉
alongside the deer, boar and aurochs	사슴, 야생 돼지 그리고 야생 소와 함께
pursued by a mounted hunter	사냥꾼에 의해 쫓긴
a speckled cat	반점이 있는 고양이
were it not for ~	~이 없다면
animal's backside	동물의 엉덩이
wear away with time	시간에 따라 마모되다
stubby tail	짧고 굵은 꼬리
unmistakable	명백한

even without this key feature	심지어 주요한 특징 없이
the creature	생명체
the totemic animal	신앙적인 동물
transform	변화시키다
environmentalism	환경보호주의
rewilding	다시 야생 상태로 돌리는 것

Paragraph 3

the mass restoration of ~	~의 대규모로 재건
damaged ecosystem	손상된 생태계
return to places	장소들로 돌아가다
denude	멸종하다
allow A to B	A를 B 하도록 허락하다
parts of the seabed	해저의 일부분
trawling and dredging	저인망
permit A to B	A가 B 하도록 허락하다
above all	무엇보다도 특히
bring back missing species	실종된 종들을 되찾다
one of the most striking findings	가장 놀라운 결과 중에 하나는
modern ecology	현대 생태 환경
predators	포식자들
behave	작용하다, 행동하다
retain	유지하다, 보유하다
drive dynamic process	동적인 과정을 진행하다
resonate	반향을 일으키다, 와닿다
create niches	틈새를 만들다
otherwise	그렇지 않으면
struggle to ~	~ 하기 위해 몸부림치다
turn out	드러나다, 판명되다
bringers of life	삶을 가져오는 자들

Paragraph 4

such findings	그러한 결과들
present	보여 주다
a big challenge	큰 문제
conservation	보호, 보존
select	선택하다
arbitrary assemblages of ~	~에 대한 임의의 집합
at great effort and expense	대단한 노력과 비용으로
prevent A from B	A가 B 하는 것으로부터 막다

as if ~	마치 ~인 것처럼
a jar of pickles	피클 한 병
let nothing in and nothing out	어떤 것도 나가고 들어오는 것을 허용 안 함
in a state of arrested development	발달 저지 상태로
be not merely	단지 ~이 아니다
ever-shifting relationships	계속 바뀌는 관계들
depend on ~	~에 좌우되다

Paragraph 5

the potential	잠재력, 가능성
even greater	훨씬 큰
commercial fishing	상업적인 어업
literature	문학
vast shoals of fish	어류의 광대한 떼
chased by fin and sperm whales	지느러미와 향유고래에 의해 쫓긴
boost catches	포획량을 촉진시키다
in the surrounding seas	주변 바다에서
insistence on ~	~에 대한 고집
scour	찾아다니다
every inch of seabed	해저 구석구석
breeding reserves	번식보호구역
damage to its own interests	그 자신의 이익에 손상을 주다

Paragraph 6

a rare example	드문 예
articulate	(생각 등을) 말로 표현하다
what they are for(against)	그들이 찬성(반대)하는 것
rather than ~	~보다
enthusiasm	열정
a inspiring vision	감동을 주는 비전
green movement	환경 운동
usual promise	일상적인 약속
less awful than ~	~보다 덜 끔찍하다
otherwise	그렇지 않으면

Paragraph 7

present threat to human beings	인간을 위협하다
prey on people	사람을 먹이로 하다
a specialist predator	전문 포식자
roe deer	노루

explode	폭발적으로 증가하다
in recent decades	최근 수십 년 동안
hold back	저지하다, 억제하다
by intensive browsing	집중적인 탐색에 의해
attempt to re-establish	복구(재건)를 시도하다
winkle out ~	~을 끌어내다
an exotic species	외래종
impenetrable plantations	들어갈 수 없는 농장들
reintroduce	재도입하다
marry well with ~	~와 잘 맞다
bring A back to ~	A를 ~로 다시 가져오다
bare and barren	불모지
deep cover	은닉, 은폐
present little risk to ~	~에게 전혀 위협을 가하지 않다
be supposed to	해야 한다
as a condition of ~	~의 조건으로서
farm subsidies	농업 보조금
out of the woods	숲에서 벗어나

Paragraph 8

several conservationists	몇몇의 보호주의자
within 20 years	20년 안에
bare hills	벌거벗은 언덕들
there is nothing extraordinary about ~	~에 대해 특별할 것이 없다
proposals	제안들
from the perspective of ~	~의 관점으로부터
re-established itself	재설립된 그 자체
triple	3배의
lucrative	이익이 되는
protect charismatic wildlife	카리스마가 있는 야생 동물을 보호하다
pay for the chance	기회에 대한 대가를 지불하다
large-scale rewilding	큰 규모의 야생 되돌리기

Paragraph 9

attitudes	태도들
preservation-jar model	보존 병 사례, 견본
even on its own terms	그 자체로도
in the highlands	산악 지대
a hint of what might be coming	무엇이 올지도 모르는 것에 대한 힌트
set up	설립하다
catalyse	촉매 작용을 하다, 촉진시키다
rarest of species	가장 희귀한 종

REVIEW

	~ 할 때이다
	사라진 토종 동물들

Paragraph 1

	시
describe hunting	
nothing seemed to fit	
an animal bone	
date from ~	
lynx	
a large spotted cat	
tasselled ears	
	가정하다
	멸종하다
	거주민들
	농사를 시작하다
	설득력 있는 증거
one and the same animal	
	제시하다
estimated extinction date	
by roughly 5,000 years	

Paragraph 2

the last glimpse	
alongside the deer, boar and aurochs	
pursued by a mounted hunter	
a speckled cat	
	~이 없다면
animal's backside	
wear away with time	시간
stubby tail	
	명백한
even without this key feature	
	생명체
the totemic animal	
	변화시키다
	환경보호주의
rewilding	

Paragraph 3

the mass restoration of ~	
	손상된 생태계
	장소들로 돌아가다
	멸종하다
	A를 B 하도록 허락하다
parts of the seabed	
trawling and dredging	
	A가 B 하도록 허락하다
	무엇보다도 특히
bring back missing species	
	가장 놀라운 결과 중에 하나는
	현대 생태계
	포식자들
behave	작용하다, 행동하다
retain	
drive dynamic process	
resonate	
create niches	
	그렇지 않으면
	~ 하기 위해 몸부림치다
turn out	
bringers of life	

Paragraph 4

such findings	
	보여 주다
	큰 문제
	보호, 보존
	선택하다
arbitrary assemblages of ~	
	대단한 노력과 비용으로
	A가 B 하는 것으로부터 막다
	마치 ~인 것처럼
a jar of pickles	
let nothing in and nothing out	
in a state of arrested development	
	단지 ~이 아니다
ever-shifting relationships	
	~에 좌우되다

Paragraph 5

the potential	
	훨씬 큰
	상업적인 어업
	문학
vast shoals of fish	
chased by fin and sperm whales	
	포획량을 촉진시키다
	주변 바다에서
	~에 대한 고집
	찾아다니다
every inch of seabed	
	번식보호구역
damage to its own interests	

Paragraph 6

	드문 예
articulate	
what they are for(against)	
rather than ~	
	열정
a inspiring vision	
	환경 운동
usual promise	
less awful than ~	
otherwise	

Paragraph 7

	인간을 위협하다
prey on people	
	전문 포식자
roe deer	
explode	
	최근 수십 년 동안
	저지하다, 억제하다
by intensive browsing	
attempt to re-establish	
winkle out ~	
	외래종

impenetrable plantations	
reintroduce	
marry well with ~	
bring A back to ~	
bare and barren	
deep cover	
	~에게 전혀 위협을 가하지 않다
be supposed to	
as a condition of ~	
	농업 보조금
out of the woods	

Paragraph 8

	몇몇의 보호주의자
	20년 안에
bare hills	
there is nothing extraordinary about ~	
	제안들
from the perspective of ~	
re-established itself	
triple	
	이익이 되는
protect charismatic wildlife	
pay for the chance	
large-scale rewilding	

Paragraph 9

attitudes	
preservation-jar model	
even on its own terms	
in the highlands	
a hint of what might be coming	
	설립하다
catalyse	
rarest of species	

PASSAGE 3
UK companies need more effective boards of directors

VOCA

boards of directors	이사회

Paragraph A

a number of ~	많은 ~
serious failure of governance	심각한 관리의 실패
that is	즉, 다시 말해서
at the highest level	가장 높은 수준에서
as well as elsewhere	다른 곳뿐만 아니라
consider radical changes	급격한 변화를 고려하다
the role of a board director	이사회 이사의 역할
financial meltdown	금융 붕괴
result in	야기하다, 초래하다
a deeper and prolonged period	심화되고 장기화된 기간
economic downturn	경기 침체
the search for explanations	이유에 대한 탐색
in the many post-mortems of the crisis	그 위기의 많은 사후 분석에서
blame	책임
spread far and wide	도처에 널리 퍼지다
regulators / central banks / auditors	규제 기관들 / 중앙은행들 / 회계 감사관들
be in the frame	틀 안에 있다, 책임이 있다
publicised failures	공표된 실패들은
be extensively picked over and examined	광범위하게 살펴지고 조사되다
in reports, inquiries and commentaries	보고서, 조사와 논평에 있어서

Paragraph B

the knock-on effect of scrutiny	조사의 연쇄 반응
the governance of companies	회사들의 관리
in general	일반적으로
an issue of intense public debate	강력한 대중 토론의 주제
increase the pressure on ~	~에 대한 압박을 증가시키다

the responsibilities of ~	~에 대한 책임
at the simplest and most practical level	가장 단순하고 실질적인 수준에서
involved in ~	~에 관련된
fufilling the demands of	~에 대한 요구를 시행하는 것
a board directorship	이사회의 지시
call into question	의문을 제기하다
the effectiveness of the classic model	전통적인 방식의 효율성
corporate governance	기업의 관리
independent non-executive directors	독립적인 비경영의 지도자
consist of ~	~을 구성하다
require board input and decisions	이사회의 조언과 결정을 요구하다
furthermore	더욱이
preparation required for ~	~을 위해 요구되어진 준비
agendas	의제, 안건
become overloaded	과부화가 되다
the time for constructive debate	건설적인 토론을 위한 시간
must necessarily be restricted	반드시 제한됨에 틀림없다
in favor of getting through the business	사업을 해내기 위해서

Paragraph C

be devolved to committees	위원회에게 양도되다
in order to ~	~을 위해서
cope with the workload	일을 해결하다
as a whole	전체적으로
be less involved in addressing	해결하는 데 덜 관련되다
it is not uncommon	그것은 일반적이다
the audit committee meeting	감사위원회 회의
last longer than ~	~보다 더 오래 지속되다
take the place of discussion	토론을 대신하다
be at the expense of real collaboration	실제의 협력을 희생하다
boxes are ticked	체크 표시가 되다
rather than ~	~보다
tackle	해결하다

Paragraph D

a radical solution	급진적 해법
work for ~	~을 위해 작용하다(유효하다)
extensive and complex	광범위하고 복잡한
the professional board	전문적 위원회
work up to three or four days	3일 또는 4일까지 일하다

dedicated staff and advisers	헌신적인 직원과 고문들
obvious risks to this	이것에 대한 분명한 위험들
establish clear guidelines	분명한 기준을 설립하다
ensure	보장하다, 확실하게 하다
step on the toes of management	경영(관리)의 심기를 건드리다
become engaged in	참여하게 되다
day-to-day	매일의
recruitment / remuneration and independence	채용 / 급료 그리고 독립
arise	발생하다, 생기다
appropriate	적절한
profession and better-informed boards	전문성과 더 견문이 넓은 이사회
the executives	임원들
have access to information	정보에 접근하다
part-time and non-executives directors	비정규 그리고 사외이사
leave A unable to	A를 할 수 없는 상태로 남기다
the latter	후자
comprehend and anticipate	이해하고 예상하다
the 2008 crash	2008년 붕괴

Paragraph E

one of the main criticisms	주요 비판들 중의 하나
focus sufficiently on ~	충분히 ~에 집중하다
longer-term matters of ~	~에 대한 장기적인 문제들
strategy, sustainability and governance	전략, 지속 가능성과 관리(지배)
instead	대신에
concentrate too much on ~	너무 ~에 집중하다
short-term financial metrics	단기적인 금융 지표
regulatory requirements	규제 요구들
the structure of the market	시장 구조
encourage	부추기다
the tyranny of quarterly reporting	분기별 보고서의 횡포
distort board decision-making	이사회의 결재(의사결정)를 왜곡하다
meet the insatiable appetite	만족할 줄 모르는 욕망을 충족하다
the trading methodology	거래 방법론
a certain kind of investor	특정 종류의 투자자
move in and out of a stock	주식을 팔고 사다
without engaging in ~	~에 참여 없이
constructive dialogue	발전적인 대화
strategy or performance	전략 또는 수행(성과)
seek a short-term financial gain	단기적인 수익을 추구하다

make worse	악화되다
the changing profile of investors	투자자들의 변화하는 태도
due to the globalisation of capital	자본의 국제화 때문에
the increasing use of ~	~의 증가하는 사용
automated trading systems	자동화 거래 시스템
corporate culture adapts	기업 문화 변화
be incentivised to ~	~을 위해 (보상금을 주어) 장려되다
meet financial goals	재정적 목적을 충족하다

Paragraph F

compensation for chief executives	최고 경영자에 대한 보상
become a combat zone	논란의 장이 되다
pitched battles	총력전
behind closed doors	비밀리에
frequently	자주
in the full glare of press attention	언론의 이목이 집중되는 가운데
in the interest of ~	~에 대한 관심이다
transparency	투명성
shareholders	주주들
use their muscle	많은 힘을 쓰다
in the area of pay	임금의 영역에서
to pressure boards	이사회에 압력을 가하기 위해서
underperforming chief executives	기대에 미치지 못하는 최고 경영자들
vote down ~	~을 거부하다
executive remuneration policies	경영자의 보상 정책들
binding votes	법적 구속력이 있는 투표
came into force	시행되다
the chair of ~	~의 의장
lonely role	외로운 역할
resign	사퇴하다
defend the enormous bonus	엄청난 보너스를 지키다
speak out against it	그것에 반대하는 의견을 말하다
in the privacy of the committee	위원회에서 사적으로

Paragraph G

financial crisis	재정적인 위기
stimulate a debate about ~	~에 대한 토론을 촉진시키다
a heightened awareness of corporate ethics	강화된 기업 윤리의 인식
trust in corporation	기업에서 신뢰
erode	침식하다, 부식하다

academics	학자들
thoughtful	사려 깊은
the morality of capitalism	자본주의의 도덕성
in all sectors	모든 분야에 있어서
widen their perspective	그들의 시각을 넓히다
encompass this issue	이 문제를 포함하다
involve a realignment of corporate goals	회사의 목표의 재편성을 포함하다
in challenging times	어려운 시기에

REVIEW

boards of directors	

Paragraph A

a number of ~	
serious failure of governance	
	즉, 다시 말해서
	가장 높은 수준으로
	다른 곳뿐만 아니라
consider radical changes	
the role of a board director	
	금융 붕괴
	야기하다, 초래하다
a deeper and prolonged period	
	경기 침체
the search for explanations	
in the many post-mortems of the crisis	
	책임
	도처에 널리 퍼지다
regulators / central banks / auditors	
be in the frame	
publicised failures	
be extensively picked over and examined	
in reports, inquiries and commentaries	

Paragraph B

	조사의 연쇄 반응
the governance of companies	
	일반적으로
an issue of intense public debate	
increase the pressure on ~	
	~에 대한 책임
at the simplest and most practical level	
	~에 관련된
fufilling the demands of	
	이사회의 지시
	의문을 제기하다
the effectiveness of the classic model	

corporate governance	
independent non-executive directors	
	구성하다
require board input and decisions	
	더욱이
preparation required for	
	의제, 안건
	과부화가 되다
the time for constructive debate	
must necessarily be restricted	
in favor of getting through the business	사업을 해내기 위해서

Paragraph C

be devolved to committees	
	~을 위해서
	일을 해결하다
	전체적으로
be less involved in addressing	
	그것은 일반적이다
the audit committee meeting	
	~보다 더 오래 지속되다
	토론을 대신하다
be at the expense of real collaboration	
boxes are ticked	
	~보다
	해결하다

Paragraph D

	급진적 해법
work for ~	
extensive and complex	
the professional board	
work up to three or four days	
dedicated staff and advisers	
obvious risks to this	
	분명한 기준을 설립하다
	보장하다, 확실하게 하다
step on the toes of management	
	참여하게 되다
day-to-day	

recruitment / remuneration and independence	
	발생하다, 생기다
	적절한
profession and better-informed boards	
	임원들
	정보에 접근하다
part-time and non-executives directors	
leave A unable to	
the latter	
	이해하고 예상하다
the 2008 crash	

Paragraph E

	주요 비판들 중의 하나
	충분히 ~에 집중하다
longer-term matters of ~	
	전략, 지속 가능성과 관리(지배)
	대신에
	너무 ~에 집중하다
short-term financial metrics	
	규제 요구들
	시장 구조
	부추기다
the tyranny of quarterly reporting	
distort board decision-making	
meet the insatiable appetite	
the trading methodology	
a certain kind of investor	
move in and out of a stock	
without engaging in ~	
constructive dialogue	
	전략 또는 수행(성과)
	단기적인 수익을 추구하다
	악화되다
the changing profile of investors	
due to the globalisation of capital	
	~의 증가하는 사용
automated trading systems	
	기업 문화 변화
be incentivised to ~	
	재정적 목적을 충족하다

Paragraph F

compensation for chief executives	
become a combat zone	
pitched battles	
behind closed doors	
	자주
in the full glare of press attention	
in the interest of ~	
	투명성
	주주들
use their muscle	
in the area of pay	
to pressure boards	
	기대에 미치지 못하는 최고 경영자들
vote down ~	
executive remuneration policies	
binding votes	
	효력을 발생하다
the chair of ~	
lonely role	
	사퇴하다
defend the enormous bonus	
speak out against it	
in the privacy of the committee	

Paragraph G

	재정적인 위기
	~에 대한 토론을 촉진시키다
a heightened awareness of corporate ethics	
trust in corporation	
	침식하다, 부식하다
	학자들
	사려 깊은
the morality of capitalism	
in all sectors	
	그들의 시각을 넓히다
encompass this issue	
involve a realignment of corporate goals	
	어려운 시기에

P A R T

02

Cambridge IELTS 13

TEST

1

PASSAGE 1
Case study: Tourism New Zealand website

VOCA

case study	사례 연구

Paragraph 1

inhabitants	거주민들
a long-haul flight	장거리 비행
the major tourist-generating market	주요한 여행객들을 발생시키는 시장
make up	구성하다
gross domestic product	국내 총생산량
the largest export sector	가장 큰 수출 분야
unlike ~	~와 달리
make products and then sell	상품을 만들고 팔다
overseas	해외의
tourism	관광 산업
bring A to B	A를 B로 데려오다
the country itself	그 나라 자체
launch a campaign	캠페인을 시작하다
communicate A to B	A를 B에게 전달하다
focus on ~	~에 집중하다
scenic beauty	경치의 아름다움
exhilarating outdoor activities	활력 있는 야외 활동들
authentic Maori culture	실제의 마오리 문화
the strongest national brands	가장 강력한 국가 브랜드

Paragraph 2

a key feature	주요한 특징
provide A with B	A에게 B를 제공하다
potential visitors	잠재적인 방문객들
a single gateway to everything	모든 것에 대한 유일한 통로
destination had to offer	관광지는 제공해야만 했다
the heart of ~	~의 핵심
a database of tourism service operators	관광 산업 서비스 제공자들의 자료
those based in New Zealand	뉴질랜드에 기반을 둔 사람들

those based abroad	해외에 기반을 둔 사람들
offer A to B	A를 B에게 제공하다
tourism- related business	관광 산업에 관련된 사업
be listed by ~	~에 의해 작성되다(목록화되다)
fill in a simple form	간단한 형식에 기입하다
specialist activity provider	전문 활동 제공자
gain a web presence	웹 보유를 획득하다
with access to an audience	독자들에게 접근할 수 있는
in addition	덧붙여서
participate businesses	사업에 참여하다
update the details	세부 사항들을 업데이트하다
on a regular basis	정기적으로
the information provided	제공된 정보
remain accurate	정확하게 유지하다
organize a scheme	계획하다
whereby	그것으로 인해
organizations appearing on the website	웹사이트에 나타나는 기관들
underwent an independent evaluation	독립적인 평가를 받다
a set of ~	일련의 ~
agreed national standard of quality	합의된 국가 품질 기준
be considered	고려되다

Paragraph 3

communicate	대화하다
carry features relating to ~	~에 관련된 특징들을 게재하다
an interview with ~	~와의 인터뷰
attract a lot of attention	많은 관심을 끌다
an interactive journey	상호적인 여행
locations chosen for blockbuster films	대형 영화를 위해 선택된 지역들
make use of ~	~을 이용하다
stunning scenery as a backdrop	배경으로서 놀라운 경치
additional features	부가적인 특징들
be added to ~	~에 덧붙여지다
independent travellers	독립 여행자들
devise their own customized itineraries	그들 스스로 맞춰진 여정을 만들다
make it easier to plan motoring holiday	자동차 여행을 계획하는 것을 쉽게 하다
catalogue	분류하다, 목록화하다
the most popular driving routes	가장 유명한 드라이브 길들
highlight	강조하다
according to the season	시즌에 따라서
indicate distance and times	거리와 시간을 보여 주다

Paragraph 4

allow A to B	A가 B 하는 것을 허락하다
bookmark	북마크하다, 기록해 두다
attractions	명소들, 볼거리들
be interested in ~	~에 관심을 가지다
view the results on a map	지도상에서 결과를 보다
suggested routes	추천된 길들
accommodation	숙박
register with the website	웹사이트에 등록하다
on the visit	방문 중에
submit	제출하다
for possible inclusion	가능한 가입을 위해

Paragraph 5

win awards for ~	~ 때문에 상을 타다
achievement and innovation	성취와 혁신
most interestingly perhaps	아마도 가장 흥미로운 것
the growth of tourism	관광 산업의 성장
impressive	놀라운
overall tourism expenditure	전반적인 관광 비용
increase by ~	~만큼 증가하다
compared to ~	~와 비교하여

Paragraph 6

set up	설립하다
create itineraries and travel packages	일정표와 여행 패키지를 만들다
suit	적합하다, 어울리다
search for ~	~을 찾다
not solely by A, but also by B	A에 의해서뿐만 아니라 B에 의해서도
by geographical location	지리학적인 위치에 의해
particular nature of the activity	그 활동의 특별한 특성
a key driver of ~	~의 주요한 원인
contribute 74% to visitor satisfaction	74%를 방문객 만족도에 기여하다
account for the remaining	나머지를 차지하다
undertake	착수하다, 하다
the more A, the more B	A 하면 할수록 더 B 하다
be interactive	상호적이다
many long-haul travelers	많은 장거리 여행객들
take home	집으로 가져가다

in addition	덧붙여서
it appear that ~	~인 것 같다
involve a few people	몇 명만 참여하다
special and meaningful	특별하고 의미 있는

Paragraph 7

a typical destination	전형적인 관광지
composed of	~로 구성되어진
it is generally perceived	일반적으로 인식되어지다
a reliable transport infrastructure	신뢰할 수 있는 교통 사회기반시설
because of the long-haul flight	장기간의 비행 때문에
as much of the country as possible	가능한 한 그 나라의 많은 것들
seen as once-in-a lifetime	일생의 한 번으로 여겨진
the underlying lessons	근본적인 교훈들
apply anywhere	어디에나 적용하다
the effectiveness of ~	~의 효율성
a strategy based on ~	~에 기초한 전략
a comprehensive and user-friendly website	포괄적이고 사용자 친화적인 웹사이트

REVIEW

case study	

Paragraph 1

	거주민들
	장거리 비행
the major tourist-generating market	
make up	
gross domestic product	
	가장 큰 수출 분야
	~와 달리
make products and then sell	
	해외의
	관광 산업
	A를 B로 데려오다
the country itself	
	캠페인을 시작하다
communicate A to B	
	~에 집중하다
	경치의 아름다움
exhilarating outdoor activities	
authentic Maori culture	
the strongest national brands	

Paragraph 2

	주요한 특징
	A에게 B를 제공하다
	잠재적인 방문객들
a single gateway to everything	
destination had to offer	
	~의 핵심
a database of tourism service operators	
those based in New Zealand	
those based abroad	
	A를 B에게 제공하다
	관광 산업에 관련된 사업
be listed by	
fill in a simple form	

specialist activity provider	
gain a web presence	
with access to an audience	
	덧붙여서
	사업에 참여하다
	세부 사항들을 업데이트하다
	정기적으로
	제공된 정보
remain accurate	
	계획하다
whereby	
organizations appearing on the website	
	독립적인 평가를 받다
a set of ~	
agreed national standard of quality	
	고려되다

Paragraph 3

	대화하다
carry features relating to ~	
	~와의 인터뷰
	많은 관심을 끌다
an interactive journey	
locations chosen for blockbuster films	
	~을 이용하다
stunning scenery as a backdrop	
	부가적인 특징들
	~에 덧붙여지다
	독립 여행자들
devise their own customized itineraries	
make it easier to plan motoring holiday	
catalogue	
the most popular driving routes	
	강조하다
	시즌에 따라서
indicate distance and times	

Paragraph 4

	A가 B 하는 것을 허락하다
bookmark	
	명소들, 볼거리들
	~에 관심을 가지다
view the results on a map	
suggested routes	
	숙박
	웹사이트에 등록하다
	방문 중에
	제출하다
for possible inclusion	

Paragraph 5

	~ 때문에 상을 타다
	성취와 혁신
most interestingly perhaps	
	관광 산업의 성장
	놀라운
overall tourism expenditure	
	~만큼 증가하다
	~와 비교하여

Paragraph 6

	설립하다
create itineraries and travel packages	
	적합하다, 어울리다
	~을 찾다
not solely by A, but also by B	
by geographical location	
particular nature of the activity	
	~의 주요한 원인
contribute 74% to visitor satisfaction	
	나머지를 차지하다
undertake	
	A 하면 할수록 더 B 하다
	상호적이다
	많은 장거리 여행객들
take home	

	덧붙여서
	~인 것 같다
involve a few people	
	특별하고 의미 있는

Paragraph 7

	전형적인 관광지
	~로 구성되어진
	일반적으로 인식되어지다
a reliable transport infrastructure	
	장기간의 비행 때문에
	가능한 한 그 나라의 많은 것들
seen as once-in-a lifetime	
	근본적인 교훈들
	어디에나 적용하다
	~의 효율성
	~에 기초한 전략
	포괄적이고 사용자 친화적인 웹사이트

PASSAGE 2
Why being bored is stimulating-and useful, too

VOCA

turn out	밝혀지다, 나타나다

Paragraph A

keep your mind on ~	~에 집중하다
time stretches out	시간이 길어지다
seem unlikely to ~	~ 할 것 같지 않다
feel better	기분이 좋아지다
define boredom	지루함을 정의하다
prove difficult	어려움을 입증하다
for a start	우선
mental states	정신적인 상태
frustration / apathy / depression / indifference	좌절 / 냉담 / 우울 / 무관심
agreement over ~	~에 대한 합의
a low-energy, flat kind of emotion	저에너지, 평범한 종류의 감정
feel agitated and restless	동요함과 불안함을 느끼다
count as boredom	지루함으로 간주되다
compare A to B	A를 B와 비교하다
motivate A to B	A에게 B 하도록 동기부여하다
stay away from certain situations	일정한 위치로부터 떨어지다
disgust	혐오감
protect A from B	A를 B로부터 보호하다
infection	전염
infectious social situations	전염성이 있는 사회적 상황들

Paragraph B

the experiences of boredom	지루함의 경험
identify	밝히다, 확인하다
five distinct types	다섯 가지 다른 유형들
calibrating / searching / reactant / apathetic	규격 / 검색 / 반응하는 / 무관심한
be plotted on two axes	두 축으로 계획되다
measure low to high arousal	낮은 자극에서 높은 자극까지 측정하다
from top to bottom	정상에서 바닥까지

positive or negative	긍정적인 또는 부정적인
intriguingly	흥미롭게도
all kinds of boredom	모든 종류의 지루함
specialize in ~	~에 특화되어 있다
of the five types	5가지 형태 중에서
the most damaging	가장 큰 피해
with its explosive combination	충격적인 조합과 함께
engage in ~	~에 참여하다
anything satisfying	만족시키는 어떤 것
feel relaxed and calm	편안함과 고요함을 느끼다
character traits	성격적 특성
predict	예상하다
be prone to ~	~ 하기 쉽다, ~ 하는 경향이 있다

Paragraph C

psychologist	심리학자
go further	더 나아가다
being bored	지루해지는 것은
make us more creative	우리를 더 창의적으로 만들다
be afraid of ~	~을 두려워하다
in actual fact	사실상
lead to amazing things	놀라운 것을 야기하다
experiments published	발표된 실험들
by copying numbers	수들을 복사함으로써
come up with ~	~을 생각해 내다
conclude	결론 내리다
a passive, boring activity	수동적이고 지루한 활동
for creativity	창의력을 위해
allow the mind to wander	그 마음을 배회하게 허용하다
go so far as to suggest	심지어 제안하기까지 하다
seek out ~	~을 찾아내다

Paragraph D

be convinced	확신하다
in a state of mind-wandering	딴생각을 하는 상태
by definition	정의에 의하면
an undesirable state	바람직하지 못한 상태
does not necessarily mean	반드시 의미하지는 않는다
adaptive	적응할 수 있는
physical pain	육체적인 고통

happen to ~	~에게 발생하다
actively cause pain	적극적으로 고통을 야기하다
evolve to help ~	~을 돕도록 진화하다
be toxic	독성이 있다
fester	악화되다
the central feature of boredom	지루함의 중요한 특징
a failure to ~	~에 대한 실패
put A into gear	A를 작동시키다
attention system	집중 시스템
an inability to focus on ~	~에 집중하는 것에 대한 무능력
go painfully slowly	천천히 고통스럽게 되다
what's more	더욱이
efforts to improve the situation	상황을 개선시키려는 노력
end up ~ing	결국 ~ 하게 되다
make A feel worse	A를 기분 나쁘게 만들다
connect with the world	세상과 연결하다
frustration and irritability	좌절과 성급함
most worryingly	가장 걱정스럽게
engage attention	주의를 기울이다
lead to a state	상태를 야기하다
no longer	더 이상 ~ 아니다

Paragraph E

explore	탐구하다
at least	적어도
come down to ~	~로 요약되다, ~에 이르다
personality	성격, 인성
boredom proneness	지루한 성향
be linked with ~	~와 관련 있다
a variety of traits	다양한 (성격상의) 특성들
be motivated by pleasure	기쁨에 의해 동기화되다
suffer particularly badly	특히 심하게 겪다
such as curiosity	호기심과 같은
be associated with ~	~와 관련 있다
a high boredom threshold	높은 지루함의 한계점
evidence	증거
has detrimental effects	해로운 영향을 가지다
come from studies	연구들로부터 오다
more or less	다소, 어느 정도
be prone to boredom	지루해하는 경향이 있다

face poorer prospects in education	교육에서 더 나쁜 전망에 직면하다
in general	일반적으로
boredom itself	지루함 그 자체
deal with ~	~을 다루다
put A in danger	A를 위험에 빠뜨리다
alleviate	완화하다
suggestion	제안
approach	접근하다
in other words	다시 말해서
get stuck in anyway	어쨌든 갇히다
avoid	피하다
for distraction	오락을 위해

Paragraph F

speculate	추측하다, 분석하다
over-connected lifestyles	과도하게 연관된 생활 방식
overstimulation	과잉 자극
instead of seeking mental stimulation	정신적인 자극을 찾는 대신에
leave A alone	A를 홀로 놔두다
engage with the world	세계와 관계 맺다
in a more meaningful way	더 의미 있는 방법에 있어

REVIEW

turn out	

Paragraph A

	~에 집중하다
time stretches out	
	~ 할 것 같지 않다
	기분이 좋아지다
define boredom	
prove difficult	
	우선
	정신적인 상태
	좌절 / 냉담 / 우울 / 무관심
agreement over	
a low-energy, flat kind of emotion	
	동요함과 불안함을 느끼다
	지루함으로 간주되다
	A를 B와 비교하다
	A에게 B 하도록 동기부여하다
stay away from certain situations	
	혐오감
	A를 B로부터 보호하다
	감염
infectious social situations	

Paragraph B

the experiences of boredom	
identify	
	다섯 가지 다른 유형들
calibrating / searching / reactant / apathetic	
be plotted on two axes	
measure low to high arousal	
from top to bottom	
	긍정적인 또는 부정적인
	흥미롭게도
all kinds of boredom	
	~에 특화되어 있다
of the five types	

the most damaging	
with its explosive combination	
	~에 참여하다
anything satisfying	
	편안함과 고요함을 느끼다
	성격적 특성
	예상하다
	~ 하기 쉽다, ~ 하는 경향이 있다

Paragraph C

	심리학자
	더 나아가다
being bored	
	우리를 더 창의적으로 만들다
	~을 두려워하다
in actual fact	
	놀라운 것을 야기하다
experiments published	
by copying numbers	
	~을 생각해 내다
	결론 내리다
a passive, boring activity	
	창의력을 위해
	그 마음을 배회하게 허용하다
go so far as to suggest	
	~을 찾아내다

Paragraph D

be convinced	
in a state of mind-wandering	
	정의에 의하면
	바람직하지 못한 상태
does not necessarily mean	
	적응할 수 있는
	육체적인 고통
	~에게 발생하다
actively cause pain	
evolve to help ~	
	독성이 있다
fester	

the central feature of boredom	
	~에 대한 실패
put A into gear	
attention system	
an inability to focus on ~	
go painfully slowly	
	더욱이
efforts to improve the situation	
	결국 ~ 하게 되다
make A feel worse	A를 기분 나쁘게 만들다
connect with the world	
	좌절과 성급함
most worryingly	
engage attention	
lead to a state	
	더 이상 ~아니다

Paragraph E

	탐구하다
	적어도
	~로 요약되다, ~에 이르다
	성격, 인성
boredom proneness	
	~와 관련 있다
	다양한 (성격상의) 특성들
	기쁨에 의해 동기화되다
suffer particularly badly	
	호기심과 같은
	~와 관련 있다
a high boredom threshold	
	증거
	해로운 영향을 가지다
	연구들로부터 오다
	다소, 어느 정도
	지루해하는 경향이 있다
face poorer prospects in education	
	일반적으로
boredom itself	
	~을 다루다
	A를 위험에 빠뜨리다

	완화하다
	제안
	접근하다
	다시 말해서
get stuck in anyway	
	피하다
	오락을 위해

Paragraph F

	추측하다, 분석하다
over-connected lifestyles	
overstimulation	
instead of seeking mental stimulation	
	A를 홀로 놔두다
engage with the world	
in a more meaningful way	

PASSAGE 3
Artificial artists

VOCA

Paragraph 1

a glowing number of ~	증가하는 많은 수의 ~
makers claim	제작자들은 주장하다
possess creative talents	창의적인 재능을 가지다
an artificial composer	인공적인 작곡가
have audiences enraptured	관객들을 황홀하게 하다
trick them into believing	그들을 속여 믿게 하다
be behind the score	그 악보 이면에 있다
artworks painted by ~	~에 의해 색칠된 예술 작품들
be hung in prestigious galleries	명성 있는 미술관에 걸려 있다

Paragraph 2

human beings	인류, 인간
perform sophisticated creative acts	정교한(세련된) 창의적인 행위를 하다
break A down into computer code	A를 분석하여 컴퓨터 코드에 넣다
human creativity	인간의 창의성
the very core of humanity	인간(인류)의 핵심
scare	겁을 주다
be worried that ~	~을 염려하다
take A away from B	A를 B로부터 가져가다
something special	특별한 무엇

Paragraph 3

to some extent	어느 정도
be familiar with ~	~에 친숙하다
computerized art	전산화된 예술
exhibited	전시되어진
pick up paintbrush	그림 붓을 집다
on its own	스스로
impressive perhaps	어쩌면 인상적인
little more than ~	불과(단지) ~인
realize	깨닫다

Paragraph 4

be keen to ~	~ 열렬히 원하다
make sure	확실히 하다
creation	창작, 제작
attract the same criticism	같은 비판을 이끌다
unlike earlier artists	이전의 예술가들과 달리
minimal direction	최소 지시
come up with ~	~을 생각해 내다
concept	개념, 의미
material	소재
run its own web searches	그 자신의 웹 검색을 운영하다
trawl through ~	~을 통해 세밀히 조사하다
display a kind of imagination	일종의 상상을 표현하다
from scratch	처음부터, 무에서부터
a series of fuzzy landscapes	일련의 흐릿한 풍경화들
depict	묘사하다
a mechanical look	기계적인 모습(모양)
such reactions	그러한 반응들
arise from ~	~에서 발생하다
people's double standards toward ~	~에 대한 사람들의 이중적 태도
software-produced and human-produced art	소프트웨어가 만든 그리고 인간이 만든 예술품
after all	결국
without referring to ~	~의 참고 없이
a certain level of imagination	일정 수준의 상상력
point out	주장하다
be true of ~	~에 적용되다
software bugs	소프트웨어의 결함들
unexpected results	기대하지 않은 결과
come out in black and white	흑백으로 나오다
thanks to a technical glitch	기술적 결함 덕택에
an eerie, ghostlike quality	무시무시한, 유령 같은 품질
the renowned	저명한
be lauded for ~	~ 때문에 칭찬을 받다

Paragraph 5

measure machine creativity	기계의 창의성을 비교하다
millennia	1천 년간의
be fascinated by the prospect	전망에 매료되다
as original and subtle as ~	~만큼 독창적이고 섬세한

so far	지금까지
come close	근접하다
composer	작곡가
invent a program	프로그램을 만들다
not only A, but also B	A뿐만 아니라, B도
create compositions	작곡을 하다
the most revered classical composers	가장 존경하는 클래식 작곡가들
including	~을 포함하는
audiences were moved to tears	관중들은 감동하여 울었다
fool A into B	A를 B로 속이다
classical music experts	클래식 음악의 전문가들
genuine	진짜의
not everyone was impressed	모두가 감동받은 것은 아니다
blast A as pseudoscience	A를 사이비 과학으로 맹비난하다
condemn A for B	A를 B라는 이유로 비난하다
deliberately vague explanation	의도적으로 애매한 설명
meanwhile	반면에, 다른 한편으로는
replicas	복제품들, 모형들
rely completely on ~	완전히 ~에 의존하다
creative impulses	창의적인 의도
be outraged with ~	~에 격분하다
punch	치다
amid such controversy	그러한 논쟁 속에서
vital databases	중요한 데이터베이스

Paragraph 6

recoil	움찔하다
provide a clue	실마리를 제공하다
assess	평가하다
participants	참가자들
beforehand	미리
tunes	곡조, 선율
rate	평가하다
tend to dislike the piece	곡을 싫어하는 경향이 있다
expect to be more objective	더 객관적이길 기대하다

Paragraph 7

prejudice	편견
suggestion	의견, 제안
reckon	생각하다

part of the pleasure	일부분의 기쁨
stem from ~	~에서 기인하다
the creative process	창조적인 과정
behind the work	작품 이면에
irresistible essence	저항할 수 없는 본질
experiments	실험들
similarly	비슷하게
wonder	궁금하다
obvious	분명한
therefore	그러므로
speculation	추측
cut short	끝나다
become increasingly complex	점점 복잡해지다
those greater depths	더 깊이 있는 것들
precisely	정확하게, 명확하게
tap into	이용하다
for inspiration	영감을 위해서
choose theme	주제를 선택하다
be meaningful to ~	~에게 의미가 있다

REVIEW

Paragraph 1

	증가하는 많은 수의 ~
makers claim	
possess creative talents	
	인공적인 작곡가
have audiences enraptured	
trick them into believing	
be behind the score	
	~에 의해 색칠된 예술 작품들
be hung in prestigious galleries	

Paragraph 2

	인류, 인간
perform sophisticated creative acts	
break A down into computer code	
	인간의 창의성
the very core of humanity	
scare	
	~을 염려하다
take A away from B	
something special	

Paragraph 3

	어느 정도
	~에 친숙하다
computerized art	
	전시되어진
pick up paintbrush	
on its own	
impressive perhaps	
little more than ~	
	깨닫다

Paragraph 4

	~을 열렬히 원하다
	확실히 하다

creation	
attract the same criticism	
unlike earlier artists	
minimal direction	
	~을 생각해 내다
	개념, 의미
	소재
run its own web searches	
trawl through ~	
display a kind of imagination	
from scratch	
a series of fuzzy landscapes	
	묘사하다
a mechanical look	
such reactions	
	~에서 발생하다
people's double standards toward ~	
software-produced and human-produced art	
	결국
without referring to ~	
	일정 수준의 상상력
	주장하다
	~에 적용되다
software bugs	
	기대하지 않은 결과
come out in black and white	
thanks to a technical glitch	
an eerie, ghostlike quality	
	저명한
be lauded for ~	

Paragraph 5

measure machine creativity	
millennia	
be fascinated by the prospect	
as original and subtile as ~	
	지금까지
	근접하다
	작곡가
	프로그램을 만들다

	A뿐만 아니라, B도
	작곡을 하다
the most revered classical composers	
including	
audiences were moved to tears	
fool A into B	
	클래식 음악의 전문가들
	진짜의
not everyone was impressed	
blast A as pseudoscience	
condemn A for B	
deliberately vague explanation	
	반면에, 다른 한편으로는
	복제품들, 모형들
	완전히 ~에 의존하다
creative impulses	
be outraged with ~	
	치다
amid such controversy	
vital databases	

Paragraph 6

recoil	
	실마리를 제공하다
	평가하다
	참가자들
	미리
tunes	
	평가하다
tend to dislike the piece	
expect to be more objective	

Paragraph 7

	편견
	의견, 제안
reckon	
part of the pleasure	
stem from ~	
the creative process	
behind the work	

irresistible essence	
	실험들
	비슷하게
	궁금하다
	분명한
	그러므로
	추측
	끝나다
become increasingly complex	
those greater depths	
	정확하게, 명확하게
	이용하다
	영감을 위해서
choose theme	
	~에게 의미가 있다

TEST

2

Bringing cinnamon to Europe

VOCA

Paragraph 1

cinnamon	계피
fragrant spice	향기로운 향신료
the inner bark of trees	나무의 안쪽 껍질
the genus cinnamomum	계피 종
be native to ~	~가 원산지이다
the Indian sub-continent	인도 아대륙
in biblical times	성서 시대에
as an ingredient	성분으로서
for anointing people's bodies	사람들의 몸에 바르기 위해
as a token indicating friendship	우정을 나타내는 징표로서
in ancient Rome	고대 로마에
mourners attending funerals	장례식에 참여하는 참가자들
to create a pleasant scent	기분 좋은 향을 만들기 위해
more often	더 자주
as an additive to food and drink	음식과 음료의 첨가제로서
could afford	여력이 있다
flavour food	음식에 맛을 내다
impress	인상을 주다
an expensive condiment	비싼 향신료
the exotic East	이국적인 동쪽
at a banquet	연회에서
a plate	접시
various spices piled upon it	그곳 위에 쌓인 다양한 향신료
as a sign of the wealth	부의 상징으로서
at his or her disposal	그 또는 그녀의 마음대로 할 수 있는
health benefits	건강상의 이점들
cure various ailments	다양한 질병을 치료하다
such as indigestion	소화불량과 같은

Paragraph 2

desire the lifestyle of the elite	엘리트들의 생활양식을 원하다
consumption	소비
led to a growth	증가로 이어지다
in demand	수요에 있어서
at that time	그 당시
be transported by Arab merchants	아랍의 상인에 의해 거래되다
guard the secret of the source	원료의 비밀을 보호하다
potential rivals	잠재적인 경쟁자들
on camels via on overland route	육로의 길을 통해 낙타로
to the Mediterranean	지중해까지
purchase	구매하다
bring it back to ~	그것을 다시 ~로 가져오다
small quantities of the spice	적은 양의 향신료
a virtual monopoly of the trade	무역의 사실상의 독점
set the price of ~	~의 가격을 정하다
exorbitantly high	터무니없이 높은
coupled with ~	~와 함께
spur the search for new routes	새로운 길을 찾으라고 자극하다
eager to take part in	참여하기를 원하다

Paragraph 3

seek the high profits	높은 이익을 추구하다
organize the cultivation of ~	~의 경작을 계획하다
people belonging to ~	~에 속하는 사람들
ethnic group	종족 집단
peel the bark off young shoots	새싹 껍질을 벗기다
in the rainy season	우기에
pliable	유연한
curl the bark into ~	껍질을 ~으로 말다
associated with ~	~에 관련된
as a form of tribute	공물의 형태로
increase production significantly	생산을 상당히 늘리다
enslave	노예로 만들다, 예속시키다
force A to B	A에게 B를 강요하다
harvest	수확하다
build a fort	요새를 만들다
enable A to B	A가 B를 가능하게 하다
develop a monopoly	독점을 발전시키다

generate very high profits	높은 이익을 발생시키다
a tenfold profit	10배 이익
over a journey of eight days	8일간의 여정을 거쳐

Paragraph 4

the Dutch	네덜란드인
arrive off the coast of ~	~의 연안에 도착하다
set their sights on ~	~을 정하다
displace	추방하다
allied themselves with ~	~와 동맹을 맺었다
in return for ~	~의 대가로
payments of ~	~의 지불
broke monopoly	독점을 깼다
overran and occupied	침략하고 차지했다
permanently expelled	영구적으로 추방했다
thereby	그것에 의하여
gain control of lucrative trade	이익이 되는 무역을 제압하다

Paragraph 5

in order to ~	~ 하기 위해서
protect their hold	지배를 보호하다
treat harshly	가혹하게 다루다
the native inhabitants	원주민들
because of the need	필요성 때문에
boost production	생산을 촉진하다
satisfy	만족시키다
ever-increasing appetite for ~	계속 증가하는 ~에 대한 욕구
alter	바꾸다
the harvesting practices	수확하는 관행
become nearly exhausted	거의 소진되다
due to	때문에
systematic stripping of the bark	껍질의 조직적인 벗김
eventually	결국에
cultivate	경작하다
supplement	보충하다
the diminishing number of wild trees	감소하는 야생 나무 수
available for use	이용하기에 유용한

Paragraph 6

displace A from B	B로부터 A를 추방하다
a low grade quality of the spice	낮은 수준의 향신료
become acceptable	받아들여지다
not only A, but also B	A뿐만 아니라 B도
become impossible	불가능하게 되다
diminish in economic potential	경제적인 가능성에 있어 감소하다
be eventually superseded by ~	결국에는 ~에 의해 대체되다
the rise of trade	무역의 증가

REVIEW

Paragraph 1

cinnamon	
fragrant spice	
the inner bark of trees	
the genus cinnamomum	
	~가 원산지이다
the Indian sub-continent	
in biblical times	
	성분으로서
for anointing people's bodies	
as a token indicating friendship	
in ancient Rome	
mourners attending funerals	
to create a pleasant scent	
	더 자주
as an additive to food and drink	
	여력이 있다
flavour food	
	인상을 주다
an expensive condiment	
the exotic East	
at a banquet	
	접시
various spices piled upon it	
	부의 상징으로서
at his or her disposal	
	건강상의 이점들
cure various ailments	
	소화불량과 같은

Paragraph 2

desire the lifestyle of the elite	
	소비
	증가로 이어지다
	수요에 있어서
	그 당시

be transported by Arab merchants	
guard the secret of the source	
	잠재적인 경쟁자들
on camels via on overland route	
to the Mediterranean	
purchases	
bring it back to ~	
small quantities of the spice	
a virtual monopoly of the trade	
	~의 가격을 정하다
	터무니없이 높은
	~와 함께
spur the search for new routes	
eager to take part in	

Paragraph 3

	높은 이익을 추구하다
organize the cultivation of ~	
people belonging to ~	
ethnic group	
peel the bark off young shoots	
	우기에
	유연한
curl the bark into ~	
	~에 관련된
as a form of tribute	
	생산을 상당히 늘리다
	노예로 만들다, 예속시키다
	A에게 B를 강요하다
	수확하다
build a fort	
	A가 B를 가능하게 하다
	독점을 발전시키다
	높은 이익을 발생시키다
a tenfold profit	
over a journey of eight days	

Paragraph 4

	네덜란드인
arrive off the coast of ~	

set their sights of ~	
	추방하다
allied themselves with ~	
	~의 대가로
broke monopoly	
overran and occupied	
permanently expelled	
thereby	
gain control of lucrative trade	

Paragraph 5

in order to ~	
protect their hold	
treat harshly	
the native inhabitants	
	필요성 때문에
	생산을 촉진하다
satisfy	
ever-increasing appetite for ~	
alter	
the harvesting practices	
	거의 소진되다
due to	
systematic stripping of the bark	
	결국에
	경작하다
	보충하다
the diminishing number of wild trees	
available for use	

Paragraph 6

	B로부터 A를 추방하다
a low grade quality of the spice	
	받아들여지다
	A뿐만 아니라 B도
	불가능하게 되다
diminish in economic potential	
be eventually superseded by ~	
	무역의 증가

PASSAGE 2
Oxytocin

VOCA

Paragraph A

oxytocin	옥시토신
a chemical	화학 물질
in the pituitary gland	뇌하수체에
focus on ~	~에 집중하다
became aware of ~	~을 알게 되다
the influence of oxytocin	옥시토신의 영향
reinforce the bonds	결속을 강화하다
between prairie voles	대초원 들쥐들
mate for life	삶을 위해 교미하다
trigger the motherly behaviour	자애로운 행동을 야기하다
newborn lambs	갓 태어난 양들
be released by women	여자들에 의해 분배되다
in childbirth	분만 중에
strengthen the attachment	애착을 강화하다
few chemicals	소수의 화학 물질들
as positive as ~	~만큼 긍정적인
be referred to ~	~라고 언급되다
one sniff of it	그것에 대한 한 번의 흡입
trusting / empathetic / generous / cooperative	믿는 / 감정이입의 / 관대한 / 협력적인
revise	바꾸다
wholly optimistic view	전적으로 긍정적인 관점
vary	다양하다
depend on ~	~에 좌우되다
the circumstances	상황들
impact (on) social interactions	사회적 관계에 영향을 주다
B as well as A	A뿐만 아니라 B

Paragraph B

emerge	나타나다
in a groundbreaking experiment	획기적인 실험에서

colleagues	동료들
ask volunteers to do an activity	참가자들에게 활동하라고 요청하다
invest money with an anonymous person	익명의 사람에게 돈을 투자하다
be guaranteed to be honest	정직한 것이 보장되다
participants	참가자들
via a nasal spray	코의 스프레이를 통해
beforehand	미리
receive a placebo instead	대신에 아첨(입에 발린 말)을 받다
human interactions	인간관계
quite a lonesome field	꽤 고립된 분야
be interested	관심이 있다
follow-up studies	다음의 연구들
become more charitable	더 관대해지다
become better at reading emotion	감정을 읽는 것을 더 잘하게 되다
communicate constructively in arguments	논쟁에서 건설적으로 대화하다
the results fuel the view ~	그 결과는 ~ 견해를 부추기다
enhance the positive aspects of ~	~의 긍정적인 측면을 강화하다

Paragraph C

after a few years	몇 년 후에
contrasting findings	대조적인 결과들
begin to emerge	나타나기 시작하다
play a competitive game	경쟁적인 게임을 하다
inhale the hormone	호르몬을 흡입하다
beat other players	다른 선수들을 이기다
felt more envy	더 부러움을 느끼다
what's more	더욱이
administer oxytocin	옥시토신을 투약하다
sharply contrasting outcomes	확실히 대조적인 결과들
depend on a person's disposition	사람의 성향에 좌우되다
improve people's ability	사람의 능력을 향상시키다
be socially adept to ~	사회적으로 ~에 능숙하다
reduce cooperation in ~	~에 있어 협력을 줄이다
subjects	피실험자들
be anxious or sensitive to rejection	거부에 대해 불안해하고 민감하다

Paragraph D

depend on ~	~에 좌우되다
interact with ~	~와 상호작용하다
studies conducted by ~	~에 의해 수행된 연구들

reveal	보여 주다
receive a dose of oxytocin	옥시토신의 복용량을 받다
become less cooperative	덜 협력적이 되다
deal with complete strangers	전혀 모르는 사람을 대하다
meanwhile	반면에
favouritism	편애
associate positive words with ~	긍정적인 단어들을 ~와 연관시키다
according to ~	~에 따르면
drive A to B	A를 B 하도록 유도하다
in social circles	사회적 집단에서
defend A from B	A를 B로부터 방어하다
outside dangers	외부의 위험들
it appears that ~	~인 것 같다
strengthen biases	편견을 강화하다
rather than ~	~보다
promote general goodwill	전반적인 선행을 촉진하다
as was previously thought	전에 생각되어진 것처럼

Paragraph E

signs of these subtleties	미묘한 점에 대한 신호들
from the start	처음부터
in almost half of ~	~의 반에서
the existing research results	존재하는 조사 결과들
certain individuals	특정한 개개인들
in certain circumstances	특정한 상황에서
take no notice of ~	~을 무시하다
such findings	그러한 연구 결과들
a more nuanced understanding	더욱 미묘한 차이가 있는 이해
propel investigations	조사들을 촉진하다
new lines	새로운 노선
the key to ~	~에 대한 핵심은
what the hormone does	그 호르몬이 무엇인지
lie in ~	~에 있다
pinpoint its core function	그의 핵심 기능을 정확히 찾아내다(보여 주다)
catalogue	목록화하다
its seemingly endless effects	그의 외관상 많은 효과들
hypotheses	가설들
mutually exclusive	상호배타적인
reduce anxiety and fear	걱정과 공포를 줄이다
motivate people to seek out	사람들이 찾도록 동기부여하다

social connections	사회적 관계
act as a chemical spotlight	화학적인 관심으로서 행동하다
shine	비추다
social clues	사회적인 단서들
a shift in posture	자세의 변화
a flicker of the eyes	눈의 깜박임
a dip in the voice	음성의 낮춤
make people more attuned to ~	사람들을 더 ~에 적응하게 하다
make us more likely to ~	우리를 더 ~ 할 거 같이 하다
improve ability	능력을 향상시키다
identify emotions	감정들을 알아보다(확인하다)
make things worse	상황을 악화시키다
be overly sensitive to ~	과도하게 ~에 민감하다
be prone to ~	~ 하기 쉽다
interpret social cues	사회적 신호(자극)를 해석하다
in the worst light	최악의 상황에서

Paragraph F

become more perplexing	복잡한 것이 되다
from octopuses to sheep	문어들부터 양까지
evolutionary roots	진화론적인 근원은
stretch back half a billion years	5억 년 전으로 이어지다
ancient molecule	고대의 미립자
co-opted	선택된
affect primitive parts of brain	두뇌의 미발달 부분에 영향을 주다
like the amygdala	편도선 같은
have many effects on ~	~에 많은 영향을 주다
once ~	일단 ~ 하면
add our higher-order thinking	우리의 고차원적 사고를 더하다
manifest in different ways	다른 방법에 있어서 나타나다
individual differences and context	개인의 다른 점들과 상황

REVIEW

Paragraph A

oxytocin	
	화학 물질
in the pituitary gland	
	집중하다
	~을 알게 되다
the influence of oxytocin	
reinforce the bonds	
between prairie voles	
mate for life	
trigger the motherly behaviour	
newborn lambs	
be released by women	
in childbirth	
strengthen the attachment	
few chemicals	
	~만큼 긍정적인
	~라고 언급되다
one sniff of it	
trusting / empathetic / generous / cooperative	
revise	
wholly optimistic view	
	다양하다
	~에 좌우되다
	상황들
	사회적 관계에 영향을 주다
	A뿐만 아니라 B

Paragraph B

	나타나다
	획기적인 실험에서
	동료들
ask volunteers to do an activity	
invest money with an anonymous person	
be guaranteed to be honest	
	참가자들

via a nasal spray	
	미리
receive a placebo instead	
	인간관계
quite a lonesome field	
	다음의 연구들
	관심이 있다
	더 관대해지다
become better at reading emotion	
communicate constructively in arguments	
the results fuel the view ~	
	~의 긍정적인 측면을 강화하다

Paragraph C

	몇 년 후에
	대조적인 결과들
	나타나기 시작하다
	경쟁적인 게임을 하다
inhale the hormone	
beat other players	
felt more envy	
	더욱이
administer oxytocin	
sharply contrasting outcomes	
	사람의 성향에 좌우되다
	사람의 능력을 향상시키다
	사회적으로 ~에 능숙하다
	~에 있어 협력을 줄이다
	피실험자들
	거부에 대해 불안해하고 민감하다

Paragraph D

	~에 좌우되다
	~와 상호작용하다
	~에 의해 수행된 연구들
	보여 주다
receive a dose of oxytocin	
	덜 협력적이 되다
	전혀 모르는 사람을 대하다

	반면에
	편애
	긍정적인 단어들을 ~와 연관시키다
	~에 따르면
	A를 B 하도록 유도하다
	사회적 집단에서
	A를 B로부터 방어하다
	외부의 위험들
	~인 것 같다
	편견을 강화하다
	~보다
promote general goodwill	
as was previously thought	

Paragraph E

signs of these subtleties	
	처음부터
in almost half of ~	
the existing research results	
	특정한 개개인들
	특정한 상황에서
take no notice of ~	
such findings	
a more nuanced understanding	
	조사들을 촉진하다
new lines	새로운 노선
	~에 대한 핵심은
what the hormone does	
	~에 있다
pinpoint its core function	
catalogue	
its seemingly endless effects	
	가설들
mutually exclusive	
	걱정과 공포를 줄이다
	사람들이 찾도록 동기부여하다
	사회적 관계
act as a chemical spotlight	
shine	
social clues	

a shift in posture	
a flicker of the eyes	
a dip in the voice	
make people more attuned to ~	
	우리를 더 ~ 할 것 같이 하다
	능력을 향상시키다
	감정들을 알아보다(확인하다)
	상황을 악화시키다
	과도하게 ~에 민감하다
	~ 하기 쉽다
interpret social cues	
	최악의 상황에서

Paragraph F

	복잡한 것이 되다
from octopuses to sheep	
evolutionary roots	
stretch back half a billion years	
ancient molecule	
	선택된
affect primitive parts of brain	
like the amygdala	
	~에 많은 영향을 주다
	일단 ~ 하면
add our higher-order thinking	
manifest in different ways	
individual differences and context	

PASSAGE 3
Making the most of trends

VOCA

experts	전문가들
give advice to managers	경영자들에게 충고를 주다

Paragraph 1

identify	확인하다, 알아보다
the major trends of the day	오늘의 주요한 동향(추세)
in the course of ~	~의 과정에 있어서
conduct research	연구를 수행하다
a number of industries	많은 산업들
fail to recognize	인식하는 데 실패하다
the less obvious but profound ways	덜 분명하지만 심오한 방법들
aspirations / attitudes / behaviors	열망 / 태도 / 태도
be true of ~	~에 적용되다
as peripheral to core markets	중심 시장에 대한 주변부로서

Paragraph 2

ignore trends	동향(유행)을 무시하다
innovation strategy	혁신 전략
adopt a wait-and-see approach	지켜보는 접근법을 채택하다
let competitors take the lead	경쟁자들을 리드하게 하다
at a minimum	최소한으로
missed profit opportunities	놓친 이익 기회들
at the extreme	극단적으로
jeopardize	위험에 빠뜨리다
by ceding to rivals	경쟁자들에게 양도함으로써
transform the industry	산업을 변화시키다
the purpose of this article	이 글의 목적
twofold	두 요소가 있는
spur managers	경영자를 자극하다
think expansively about ~	~에 대해 광범위하게 생각하다
value propositions	가치 제안들(문제들)
engender	불러일으키다

new value propositions	새로운 가치 제안(문제)
provide high-level advice	높은 수준의 조언을 제공하다
product development personnel	제품 개발 인력
adept at ~	~에 능숙한
analyzing and exploiting	분석과 활용하는 것

Paragraph 3

strategy	전략
known as ~	~로서 알려진
infuse and augment	주입과 증대
retain	보유하다, 유지하다
most of the attributes and functions	대부분 속성과 기능들을
existing products	기존에 있는 상품들
add others	다른 것들을 추가하다
address the needs and desires	필요성과 욕구들을 해결하다
unleashed by a major trend	주요한 유행에 의해 발생된
a case in point	이점에서 한 사례
the Poppy range of handbags	Poppy(양귀비 꽃) 분야의 핸드백을
in response to ~	~에 대한 반응으로
the economic downturn	경제적 침체
opulence and luxury	화려함과 호화로움
the most obvious reaction to ~	~에 대한 가장 분명한 반응
lower prices	가격을 낮추다
risk cheapening	품질을 떨어뜨리는 위험이다
instead	대신에
initiate a consumer-research project	소비자 조사 계획을 추진하다
reveal	보여 주다
be eager to ~	~ 하는 것을 열렬히 바라다
lift A out of tough times	힘든 시기에서 A를 벗어나게 하다
insights	식견, 통찰
launch the lower-priced Poppy	낮은 가격의 Poppy를 출시하다
in vibrant colors	생생한 색들
more youthful and playful	더 젊고 명랑한
conventional products	전통적인 상품들
the sub-brand	하위 브랜드
avert an across-the-board price cut	전반적인 가격 인하를 피하다
in contrast to ~	~와 대조적으로
respond to recession	불황에 대응하다
by cutting prices	가격 인하에 의해
the customer mindset	소비자들의 마음가짐(사고방식)
innovation and renewal	혁신과 재건

Paragraph 4

a further example of ~	~에 대한 추가 예
concerns about ~	~에 대한 걱정
the environment	환경
with that in mind	그것을 염두에 두고
retailers	소매점들, 유통 업체들
demonstrate	보여 주다
commitment to ~	~에 대한 헌신
by involving consumers	소비자들을 참여시킴으로써
tangible results	분명히 보이는 결과들
accumulate	모으다
reusing bags / recycling cans	재사용 가방, 재활용 캔들
home-insulation materials	가정 절연 물질들
be redeemed for cash	현금으로 여겨지다
abandon	버리다
traditional retail offerings	전통적인 소매 물건들
augment its business with ~	~과 함께 사업을 증가시키다
thereby	그것에 의해
infuse its value proposition	그의 가치 제안(문제)을 불어넣다
with a green streak	녹색 경향(환경)을 가지고

Paragraph 5

a more radical strategy	더 급진적인 전략
combine and transcend	조합하고 능가하다
entail	수반하다, 필요로 하다
combine A with B	A를 B와 조합하다
attributes	속성, 특질
address changes	변화들을 해결하다
arising from a trend	유행으로부터 발생하는
to create a novel experience	새로운 경험을 만들어 내다
land the company in ~	~에 회사를 두다
at first glance	언뜻 보기에
incorporate A into B	A를 B에 통합시키다
a seemingly irrelevant trend	겉보기에 관련이 없는 추세
core offerings	주요한 제품들
sound like ~	~처럼 들리다
be hardly worthwhile	거의 가치가 없다
integrate A into B	A를 B에 포함하다
the digital revolution	디지털 혁신

reputation for ~	~에 대한 평판
high-performance athletic footwear	고성능 운동선수의 운동화
team up with ~	~와 협력하다
launch	출시하다
a digital sports kit	디지털 운동장비
comprise sensor	센서를 포함하다
attach to ~	~에 부착하다
a wireless receiver	무선 수신기
connect to ~	~와 연결하다
combine A with B	A와 B를 결합하다
move from A to B	A를 B로 이동시키다
a focus on athletic apparel	운동복에 집중
a new plane of engagement with ~	~와 참여하는 새로운 수준

Paragraph 6

a third approach	세 번째 접근법은
know as ~	~로서 알려진
counteract and reaffirm	대응(반박)하고 재확인하다
involve	포함하다
stress the values	가치 기준을 강조하다
associated with the category	항목과 관련되어진
allow A to B	A가 B 하는 것을 허락하다
oppose	반대하다
at least temporarily	적어도 일시적으로
escape from ~	~로부터 벗어나다
the aspects of trends	유행의 측면
view as undesirable	바람직하지 않은 것으로 보다
accomplish	성취하다
physical play	신체놀이
counteract	대항하다, 반대로 작용하다
the widely perceived negative impacts	널리 인식된 부정적인 영향들
digital gaming devices	디지털 게임 장치들
handheld games	휴대용 게임들
feature	특징을 가지다
a host of exciting interactive games	다수의 즐거운 상호적인 게임들
advanced 3D graphics	발전된 3D 그래픽들
set it apart	그것을 구별하다
incorporate	결합하다
the traditional physical component	전통적인 신체적 구성요소
contain a pedometer	만보계를 포함하다

track and award points	추적하고 포인트를 주다
enhance various virtual skills	다양한 가상 기술들을 강화하다
cater to kids' huge desire	아이들의 거대한 욕망에 맞추다
counter the negatives	부적적인 것들을 좌절시키다, 부정적인 것들에 대응하다
associations with ~	~와 관련성
lack of exercise and obesity	운동 부족과 비만

Paragraph 7

once	일단
gain perspective on ~	~에 대한 시각을 얻다
trend-related changes	유행과 관련된 변화
in opinions and behaviors	의견과 행동에 있어서
innovation strategies	혁신적인 전략들
pursue	추구하다, 밀고 나가다
consumers influenced by the trend	유행에 의한 영향들 받는 소비자들
allow A to B	A가 B 하는 것을 허락하다
reinvigorate	활기를 되찾게 하다
analysis	분석
reveal an interesting disparity	흥미로운 차이를 보이다
transcend	초월하다
integrate	통합하다
clash with ~	~와 충돌하다
undesired outcomes	바라지 않은 결과들
reaffirm	재확인하다
the core values	주요한 가치 기준

Paragraph 8

perceive	인지하다
shape	형성하다
present firms with A	회사들에게 A를 제시하다(보여 주다)
unique opportunities for growth	성장을 위한 특별한 기회들을

REVIEW

	전문가들
give advice to managers	

Paragraph 1

identify	
the major trends of the day	
	~의 과정에 있어서
	연구를 수행하다
	많은 산업들
fail to recognize	
the less obvious but profound ways	
aspirations / attitudes / behaviors	
	~에 적용되다
as peripheral to core markets	

Paragraph 2

ignore trends	
	혁신 전략
adopt a wait-and-see approach	
let competitors take the lead	
	최소한으로
missed profit opportunities	
	극단적으로
jeopardize	
by ceding to rivals	
	산업을 변화시키다
the purpose of this article	
twofold	
spur managers	
think expansively about ~	
value propositions	
	불러일으키다
new value propositions	
provide high-level advice	
product development personnel	
	~에 능하다
analyzing and exploiting trends	

Paragraph 3

	전략
known as ~	
infuse and augment	
	보유하다, 유지하다
most of the attributes and functions	
existing products	
	다른 것들을 추가하다
address the needs and desires	
unleashed by a major trend	
a case in point	
the Poppy range of handbags	
	~에 대한 반응으로
	경제적 침체
opulence and luxury	
the most obvious reaction to ~	
	가격을 낮추다
risk cheapening	
	대신에
initiate a consumer-research project	
	보여 주다
	~ 하는 것을 열렬히 바라다
lift A out of tough times	
	식견, 통찰
launch the lower-priced Poppy	
in vibrant colors	
more youthful and playful	
	전통적인 상품들
	하위 브랜드
avert an across-the-board price cut	
	~와 대조적으로
respond to recession	
by cutting prices	
the customer mindset	
	혁신과 재건

Paragraph 4

a further example of ~	
consumers' growing concerns about ~	

	환경
with that in mind	
	소매점들, 유통 업체들
	보여 주다
	~에 대한 헌신
by involving consumers	
tangible results	
accumulate	
reusing bags / recycling cans	
home-insulation materials	
be redeemed for cash	
	버리다
traditional retail offerings	
augment its business with ~	
thereby	
infuse its value proposition	
with a green streak	

Paragraph 5

	더 급진적인 전략
combine and transcend	
entail	
	A를 B와 조합하다
	속성, 특질
	변화들을 해결하다
	유행으로부터 발생하는
	새로운 경험을 만들어 내다
land the company in ~	
	언뜻 보기에
incorporate A into B	
a seemingly irrelevant trend	
	주요한 제품들
sound like ~	
	거의 가치가 없다
	A를 B에 포함하다
	디지털 혁신
	~에 대한 평판
high-performance athletic footwear	
	~와 협력하다
	출시하다

a digital sports kit	
comprise sensor	
	~에 부착하다
a wireless receiver	
connect to ~	
	A와 B를 결합하다
move from A to B	
a focus on athletic apparel	
a new plane of engagement with ~	

Paragraph 6

	세 번째 접근법은
	~로서 알려진
counteract and reaffirm	
involve	
stress the values	가치 기준을 강조하다
associated with the category	
	A가 B 하는 것을 허락하다
	반대하다
	적어도 일시적으로
escape from ~	
the aspects of trends	
view as undesirable	
	성취하다
physical play	
the widely perceived negative impacts	
digital gaming devices	
	휴대용 게임들
	특징을 가지다
a host of exciting interactive games	
advanced 3D graphics	
set it apart	
	결합하다
the traditional physical component	
contain a pedometer	
track and award points	
enhance various virtual skills	
cater to kids' huge desire	
counter the negatives	
associations with ~	
	운동 부족과 비만

Paragraph 7

once	
gain perspective on	
	유행과 관련된 변화
in opinions and behaviors	
innovation strategies	
	추구하다, 밀고 나가다
consumers influenced by the trend	
	A가 B 하는 것을 허락하다
	활기를 되찾게 하다
	분석
reveal an interesting disparity	
	초월하다
	통합하다
clash with ~	
undesired outcomes	
	재확인하다
the core values	

Paragraph 8

	인지하다
	형성하다
present firms with A	
unique opportunities for growth	

TEST

3

The coconut palm

VOCA

Paragraph 1

for millennia	수천 년 동안
be central to ~	~의 중심이다
on the other hand	다른 한편으로는
exotic and unusual	이국적이고 특별한
rare	드문
merchant	상인
apparently	분명하게
palm-fringed tropical beaches	야자나무가 둘러싼 열대 지방 해변들
cliches	진부한 것들, 상투적인 것들
fizzy drinks	탄산음료들

Paragraph 2

typically	전형적으로
envisage A as B	A를 B로 상상하다
brown cannonballs	갈색 구형 포탄들
provide	제공하다
sweet white flesh	달콤하고 흰 과육
a smooth, slender, grey trunk	부드럽고 가늘고 회색 줄기
an important source of timber	목재의 중요한 자원
a replacement for	~을 위한 대체품
endangered hardwoods	멸종 위기 활엽수
in the furniture construction industry	가구 건설업에서
be surmounted by ~	~의해 덮여 있다(얹혀 있다)
a rosette of leaves	장미 모양의 잎들
hard veins	딱딱한 잎맥들
be used to brushes	붓으로 사용되다
be stripped away	벗겨지다
immature	다 자라지 못한
be tightly clustered together	빽빽하게 무리지다
stems	줄기들

be tapped for their sap	그들의 수액을 위해 이용되다
be reduced by boiling	끓여서 줄어들다

Paragraph 3

as many as seventy fruits	70개의 열매만큼
weigh	무게가 나가다
layers	층들
a waterproof outer layer	방수가 되는 외층
a fibrous layer	섬유 층
numerous uses	수많은 사용들
manufacture	만들다
the woody innermost layer	나무의 가장 안쪽 층
prominent	두드러진, 뛰어난
seed	씨앗
obtain from ~	~로부터 얻다
charcoal	숯
B as well as A	A뿐만 아니라 B도
cooking fuel	취사 연료
broken in half	반으로 나눠진
be used as bowls	그릇으로 쓰이다

Paragraph 4

nutrients	영양소들
initially	초기에
endosperm	배젖
a sweetish liquid	약간 단 액체
encourage A to B	A가 B 하도록 권장하다
grow more rapidly	급격하게 자라다
produce higher yields	많은 생산량을 생산하다
as the fruit matures	열매가 성숙함에 따라서
solidify	굳어지다, 응고하다
fat-rich	지방이 풍부한
edible flesh or meat	먹을 수 있는 과육 또는 알맹이
cosmetic	화장품
a derivative of ~	~의 파생물
acquire strategic importance	전략적인 중요성을 갖다
in a quite difference sphere	아주 다른 국면에서
nitroglycerin-based invention	니트로글리세린에 기초한 발명

Paragraph 5

biology	생물학
appear to ~	~인 것 같다
the maritime voyagers	해상 항해자들
coastal colonizers	연안의 식민자들
energy-rich fruits	에너지가 풍부한 열매들
float in water	물에 뜨다
tolerate salt	소금에 내성이 있다(견디다)
remain viable indefinitely	무한정으로 생존을 유지하다
be no longer able to germinate	더 이상 발아할 수 없다
literally	사실상, 실제로
cast onto desert island shores	무인도의 해안가에 던져지다
little more than ~	불과 ~인
exposed to the full glare of tropical sun	열대 태양의 눈부신 빛에 노출된
germinate and root	발아하고 뿌리를 내리다
air pocket	공기 주머니(공기가 가득한 곳)
solidify	굳어지다, 굳히다
protect the embryo	수정란을 보호하다
in addition	덧붙여서
the fibrous fruit wall	섬유질의 열매 벽
during the voyage	항해 동안
stores moisture	수분을 저장하다
be taken up by ~	~에 의해 흡수된

Paragraph 6

debate over the origins of ~	~의 기원에 대한 논쟁
explorers	탐험자들
human migration patterns	인간의 이주 형태
reveal	보여 주다
be likely to ~	~ 할 것 같다
move from A to B	A에서 B로 이동하다
the subject of ~	~의 대상
diametrically opposed origins	전혀 다른 반대되는 기원들
be native to ~	~가 원산지이다
a large degree of coconut diversity	많은 코코넛의 다양성
evidence of millennia of human use	인간 사용 1천 년의 증거
there are no relatives growing in the wild	야생에서 자라는 동류의 것들이 없다
close coconut relatives	밀접한 코코넛 동류들
indigenous	토착의, 고유한

have led to	이어져 왔다
the intriguing suggestion	재미있는 제안
be dispersed from ~	~로부터 분산되다

REVIEW

Paragraph 1

for millennia	
be central to ~	
	다른 한편으로는
	이국적이고 특별한
	드문
	상인
	분명하게
palm-fringed tropical beaches	
	진부한 것들, 상투적인 것들
	탄산음료들

Paragraph 2

	전형적으로
	A를 B로 상상하다
brown cannonballs	
	제공하다
sweet white flesh	
a smooth, slender, grey trunk	
an important source of timber	
a replacement for	
endangered hardwoods	
in the furniture construction industry	
be surmounted by	
a rosette of leaves	
hard veins	
be used to brushes	
	벗겨지다
	다 자라지 못한
be tightly clustered together	
	줄기들
be tapped for their sap	
be reduced by boiling	

Paragraph 3

as many as seventy fruits	
	무게가 나가다
layers	
a waterproof outer layer	
a fibrous layer	
	수많은 사용들
manufacture	
the woody innermost layer	
	두드러진, 뛰어난
	씨앗
	~로부터 얻다
	숯
	A뿐만 아니라 B도
	취사 연료
broken in half	
be used as bowls	

Paragraph 4

nutrients	
	초기에
endosperm	
a sweetish liquid	
	A가 B 하도록 권장하다
	급격하게 자라다
	많은 생산량을 생산하다
	열매가 성숙함에 따라서
	굳어지다, 응고하다
	지방이 풍부한
edible flesh or meat	
	화장품
a derivative of ~	
acquire strategic importance	
in a quite difference sphere	
nitroglycerin-based invention	

Paragraph 5

	생물학
	~인 것 같다
the maritime voyagers	
coastal colonizers	
	에너지가 풍부한 열매들
float in water	
tolerate salt	
remain viable indefinitely	
be no longer able to germinate	
	사실상, 실제로
cast onto desert island shores	
	불과 ~인
exposed to the full glare of tropical sun	
germinate and root	
air pocket	
protect the embryo	
	덧붙여서
the fibrous fruit wall	
during the voyage	
stores moisture	
be taken up by ~	

Paragraph 6

debate over the origins of ~	
	탐험자들
human migration patterns	
	보여 주다
	~ 할 것 같다
	A에서 B로 이동하다
	~의 대상
diametrically opposed origins	
	~가 원산지이다
a large degree of coconut diversity	
evidence of millennia of human use	
there are no relatives growing in the wild	
close coconut relatives	
	토착의, 고유한
have led to	
the intriguing suggestion	
	~로부터 분산되다

PASSAGE 2
How baby talk gives infant brains a boost

VOCA

Paragraph A

the typical way of ~	~에 대한 전형적인 방법
talk to ~	~에게 말을 걸다
high-pitched / exaggerated / repetitious	높고 날카로운 / 과장된 / 반복적인
a source of fascination	마음을 사로잡는 요소
linguists	언어학자들
impact on learning	배우는 것에 대한 영향
develop their hearing	청각을 발전시키다
in the womb	자궁에서
prompt A to B	A가 B 하도록 야기하다
pregnant bellies	임산부의 배
as early as 10 weeks before being born	태어나기 10주 전
gather the basic building blocks	기본적인 구성 요소를 모으다
family's native tongue	가족의 모국어

Paragraph B

early language exposure	이른 언어 노출
have benefits to the brain	뇌에 이점들을 가지다
for instance	예를 들어
raised in bilingual homes	이중 언어 가정에서 길러진
be better at ~	~을 잘하다
how to prioritize information	정보를 우선시하는 방법
absurd sound	황당한(말도 안 되는) 소리
infant-directed speech	유아 주도 말
explore	연구하다, 탐구하다
behind baby talk	베이비 토크 이면에

Paragraph C

as often as mothers	엄마만큼 자주
in the same ways	똑같은 방법에 있어서
according to a new study	새로운 연구에 따르면

colleagues	동료들
equip A with B	A에게 B로 갖추다
recoding devices	녹음 장치들
speech-recognition software	음성 인식 소프트웨어
interact with youngsters	어린이들과 교류하다
during a normal day	평일 동안
do exactly what you'd expect	당신이 기대하는 것을 정확히 하다
many times over	몇 번이나 되풀이하여
raise their pitch or fundamental frequency	음색 또는 기본적인 빈도수를 높이다
be rooted in ~	~에 원인이 있다
what is called	이른바, 소위
the bridge hypothesis	교량 가설
date back to ~	~까지 거슬러 올라가다
less familial language	덜 가족의 언어
provide A with B	A에게 B를 제공하다
a bridge to the kind of speech	일종의 언어의 가교
in public	사람들이 있는 데서, 공개적으로
get to practice	실행하다
a certain kind of speech	특정 종류의 말
a wider repertoire	더 넓은 범위

Paragraph D

conversations between A and B	A와 B의 대화들
fit A with B	A에게 B를 착용시키다
audio-recording vests	오디오 녹음 조끼
capture language and sound	언어와 소리를 담다
the more A, the more B	A 하면 할수록 더욱 더 B 하다
begin to babble	중얼거리기 시작하다
frequent	빈번한
drastically boost vocabulary	급격히 단어를 늘리다
regardless of ~	~에 상관없이
socioeconomic status	사회경제적인 위치
listen to ~	~을 듣다
adult talk or standard speech	성인 말이나 표준 화법
matter whether ~	~인지 아닌지 중요하다
in a one-on-one context	일대일 상황으로
talk one-on-one	일대일로 이야기하다
the more A, the more B	A 하면 할수록, 더 B 하다
later in life	나중에

Paragraph E

pair	둘씩 짝을 이루다
with their own kind	자신의 또래들과
seem to like	좋아하는 것 같다
rather than ~	~보다
such a universal tool	그러한 보편적인 도구
play repeating vowel sounds	반복된 모음 소리를 하다
a special synthesizing device	특별한 합성 기계
mimicked sounds	소리를 흉내 내다
the impact of the auditory cues	청각 신호들의 영향
observe	관찰하다
measure	측정하다
hold the infants' attention	유아의 관심을 사로잡다
induce more reactions	더 반응들을 유도하다
approximate ~	~를 흉내내다
theorize	설명하다, 이론을 세우다
attraction to other infant sounds	다른 유아의 소리에 대한 관심
launch the learning process	배우는 과정을 시작하다
lead to speech	말로 유도하다
some property of the sound	소리의 특성
draw attention	관심을 끌다
be interested in ~	~에 관심이 있다
focus on ~	~에 집중하다
speculate	추측하다, 분석하다
catch their attention	그들의 관심을 사로잡다
recognize A as B	A를 B로서 인식하다

Paragraph F

in a study published in ~	~에 발표된 연구에서
a total of 57 babies	전체 57명의 아이들
slightly different age groups	약간 다른 연령의 그룹들
a number of syllables	많은 음절들
a non-native tongue	외국어
be placed in a brain-activation scanner	뇌 활동 스캐너에 놓이다
guide the motor movements	운동을 지도하다(이끌다)
prompt A to B	A를 B 하게 야기하다
practice their language skills	그들의 언어 기술을 연습하다
activation	활성화
significant	중요한

be engaged in ~	~에 관련되다
talk back right from the start	시작부터 바로 말에 대꾸하다
figure out	알아내다
co-author	공동 작가
interesting finding	흥미로운 결과
regardless of ~	~와 상관없이
compared to ~	~와 비교해서
uncover a process	과정을 밝히다
recognize differences	차이점을 인지하다

REVIEW

Paragraph A

the typical way of ~	
	~에게 말을 걸다
high-pitched / exaggerated / repetitious	
a source of fascination	
	언어학자들
impact on learning	
develop their hearing	
in the womb	
	A가 B 하도록 야기하다
pregnant bellies	
as early as 10 weeks before being born	
gather the basic building blocks	
family's native tongue	

Paragraph B

	이른 언어 노출
have benefits to the brain	
	예를 들어
raised in bilingual homes	
	~을 잘하다
how to prioritize information	
	황당한(말도 안 되는) 소리
infant-directed speech	
	연구하다, 탐구하다
	베이비 토크 이면에

Paragraph C

as often as mothers	
	똑같은 방법에 있어서
	새로운 연구에 따르면
	동료들
	A에게 B로 갖추다
	녹음 장치들
speech-recognition software	
	어린이들과 교류하다

	평일 동안
do exactly what you'd expect	
many times over	
raise their pitch or fundamental frequency	
be rooted in ~	
	이른바, 소위
the bridge hypothesis	
date back to ~	
	덜 가족의 언어
	A에게 B를 제공하다
a bridge to the kind of speech	
	사람들이 있는 데서, 공개적으로
get to practice	
a certain kind of speech	
a wider repertoire	

Paragraph D

	A와 B의 대화들
	A에게 B를 착용하다
audio-recording vests	
capture language and sound	
	A 하면 할수록 더욱더 B 하다
begin to babble	
	빈번한
drastically boost vocabulary	
	~에 상관없이
	사회경제적인 위치
	~을 듣다
adult talk or standard speech	
	~인지 아닌지 중요하다
in a one-on-one context	
talk one-on-one	
	A 하면 할수록, 더 B하다
later in life	

Paragraph E

	둘씩 짝을 이루다
	자신의 또래들과
seem to like	
	~보다

such a universal tool	
play repeating vowel sounds	
a special synthesizing device	
mimicked sounds	
the impact of the auditory cues	
	관찰하다
	측정하다
hold the infants' attention	
induce more reactions	
	~를 흉내내다
	설명하다, 이론을 세우다
attraction to other infant sounds	
launch the learning process	
lead to speech	
some property of the sound	
	관심을 끌다
	~에 관심이 있다
	~에 집중하다
	추측하다, 분석하다
	그들의 관심을 사로잡다
	A를 B로 인식하다

Paragraph F

in a study published in ~	
a total of 57 babies	
slightly different age groups	
a number of syllables	
	외국어
be placed in a brain-activation scanner	
guide the motor movements	
prompt A to B	
	그들의 언어 기술을 연습하다
	활성화
	중요한
	~에 관련되다
talk back right from the start	
	알아내다
co-author	
interesting finding	
	~와 상관없이

	~와 비교해서
uncover a process	
	차이점을 인지하다

PASSAGE 3
Whatever happened to the Harappan Civilisation?

VOCA

shed light on ~	~을 분명히 하다
the disappearance of an ancient society	고대 사회의 멸종

Paragraph A

flourish	번창하다
be abandoned	버려지다
a sophisticated Bronze Age	수준 높은 석기 시대
megacity	거대도시
luxury craft products	고급스러운 공예품들
and yet	그럼에도, 그런데도
have left almost no depictions	묘사할 것들이 남아 있지 않다
lack of self-imagery	스스로의 이미지 부족
at a time	동시에
carve and paint	조각하고 그리다
representations of themselves	자신들의 표현
all over their temples	모든 그들의 사원들

Paragraph B

plenty of archaeological evidence	많은 고고학적인 증거
the rise of Harappan civilisation	문명의 발달(부상)
but relatively little about its fall	상대적으로 붕괴에 대해 거의 없는
archaeologist	고고학자
baths / craft workshops / palaces / halls	욕실들 / 공예작업실들 / 궁전들 / 강당들
laid out in distinct sectors	별개의 구역에 배치된
be arranged in blocks	벽돌로 정리되다(만들어지다)
narrow alleyways	좁은 골목길들
drainage systems	하수 체계
a thriving civilisation	번영하는 문화
a transformation	변화

went uncleaned	더러워졌다
ritual structures	종교의식 건축물들
fall out of use	쓰이지 않게 되다
final demise	최종 종말
a millennium	천년
large-scale cities	대규모 도시들

Paragraph C

claim	주장하다
glacier-fed rivers	빙하가 흐르는 강들
dramatically affect	크게 영향을 주다
the water supply and agriculture	물 공급과 농업
cope with	해결하다
an increasing population	증가하는 인구
exhaust their resource base	그들의 자원 기반을 소모시키다
break down	무너지다
succumb to ~	~에 굴복하다
invasion and conflict	침입과 마찰
climate change	기후 변화
cause an environmental change	환경적인 변화를 야기하다
food and water provision	음식과 물 공급
it is unlikely that ~	~일 것 같지 않다
a single cause	단 하나의 원인
the decline of the civilisation	문명의 쇠퇴
have had little solid evidence	분명한 증거가 없어 왔다
most of the key elements	대부분의 중요한 원인들
archaeological debate	고고학적인 논의
well-argued speculation	잘 논의된 추측

Paragraph D

team led by ~	~에 의해 이끌어진 팀
in their investigations	그들의 조사에서
the archaeological sites	고고학적인 장소들
be supposed to be	존재할 것으로 여겨지다
completely alter	완전히 바꾸다
be inhabited in the past	과거에 거주되다
carry out a survey of ~	~에 대한 연구를 수행하다
be settled	정착되다
in relation to ~	~와 관련해서
inaccuracy in ~	~에 있어 부정확함

the published geographic locations	공표된 지질학적인 위치들
ancient settlements	고대 정착지들
range from A to B	A로부터 B 영역까지
attempts to use	이용하려는 시도들
the existing data	존재하는 데이타
fundamentally flawed	근본적으로 결함이 있는
over the course of ~	~의 과정에 걸쳐서
several seasons of fieldwork	몇 시즌의 현장 연구
an astonishing 198 settlement sites	놀라운 198개 정착지들
be previously unknown	전에 알려지지 않다

Paragraph E

the first definitive evidence	첫 번째 결정적인 증거
affect	영향을 주다
the plains of ~	~의 평원
be known to ~	~로 알려진
gather shells of snails	달팽이 껍질을 모으다
the sediments of ~	~에 대한 침전물
geochemical analysis	지구화학적 분석
as a means of ~	~에 대한 수단으로써
trace the climate history of the region	그 지역의 기후의 역사를 추적하다
be likely to ~	~ 할 것 같다
summer monsoon	여름 우기
an abrupt change	갑작스런 변화
the amount of evaporation	증발의 양
exceed the rainfall	강우를 초과하다
indicative of a drought	가뭄을 표시하는
the weakening of ~	~에 대한 악화
last	지속하다
recover to the previous conditions	예전 조건으로 복구하다

Paragraph F

it has long been thought that ~	~을 오랫동안 생각해 오고 있다
Bronze Age civilisations	석기 문명
at a similar time	비슷한 시기에
a global-scale climate event	세계적 규모의 기후 사건(추이)
being seen as the cause	그 원인으로 보여지는
local-scale processes	지역 규모의 과정들
the real archaeological interest	실제의 고고학적인 관심
lie in understanding	이해에 있다

the vast area of ~	~의 방대한 영역
variable weather systems	다양한 기후 시스템
essential	필수적인
obtain more climate data	더 기후 자료들을 얻다
close to ~	~에 가까운

Paragraph G

details of ~	~에 대한 세부 사항들
how people led their lives	어떻게 그들의 삶을 이어 갔었는지
analyse grains cultivated at the time	그 당시에 제배된 곡물들을 분석하다
work out whether ~	~인지 아닌지 연구하다
under extreme conditions of water stress	물위기의 극한 상황에서
adjust the combinations of crops	작물의 조합에 순응하다
look at whether ~	~인지 아닌지 연구하다
the types of pottery	도자기 형태들
other aspects of their material culture	물질 문화의 다른 측면들
be distinctive to ~	~에 구별이 되다, ~에 독특하다
give us insight into ~	우리에게 ~에 대한 통찰력을 주다
interactive network	상호적인 관계
be involved in ~	~에 관여하다(참여하다)

Paragraph H

be in a unique position	특별한 위치에 있다
investigate	조사하다
respond to ~	~에 대해 반응하다
environmental pressure and threats	환경적 압박과 위협들
engage with the public	대중과 교류하다
relevant	관련된
administrative bodies	행정부 단체들
proactive in issues	문제들에 있어 더 적극적인
such as ~	~와 같은
the management and administration	관리와 행정
the balance of urban and rural development	도시와 시골 발전의 균형
preserve cultural heritage	문화유산을 보호하다

REVIEW

shed light on ~	
the disappearance of an ancient society	

Paragraph A

	번창하다
	버려지다
a sophisticated Bronze Age	
	거대도시
luxury craft products	
and yet	
have left almost no depictions	
lack of self-imagery	
	동시에
carve and paint	
representation of themselves	
all over their temples	

Paragraph B

plenty of archaeological evidence	
	문명의 발달(부상)
but relatively little about its fall	
	고고학자
baths / craft workshops / palaces / halls	
laid out in distinct sectors	
be arranged in blocks	
narrow alleyways	
drainage systems	
	번영하는 문화
	변화
went uncleaned	
ritual structures	
fall out of use	
	최종 종말
	천년
	대규모 도시들

Paragraph C

	주장하다
glacier-fed rivers	
	크게 영향을 주다
	물 공급과 농업
	해결하다
	증가하는 인구
exhaust their resource base	
break down	
	~에 굴복하다
	침입과 마찰
	기후 변화
	환경적인 변화를 야기하다
	음식과 물 공급
	~일 것 같지 않다
	단 하나의 원인
	문명의 쇠퇴
have had little solid evidence	
most of the key elements	
	고고학적인 논의
well-argued speculation	

Paragraph D

team led by ~	
in their investigations	
	고고학적인 장소들
be supposed to be	
	완전히 바꾸다
be inhabited in the past	
	~에 대한 연구를 수행하다
	정착되다
	~와 관련해서
inaccuracy in ~	
the published geographic locations	
	고대 정착지들
	A로부터 B 영역까지
attempts to use	
the existing data	
be fundamentally flawed	

over the course of ~	
several seasons of fieldwork	
an astonishing 198 settlement sites	
be previously unknown	

Paragraph E

the first definitive evidence	
	영향을 주다
	~의 평원
	~로 알려진
gather shells of snails	
the sediments of ~	
	지구화학적 분석
	~에 대한 수단으로써
trace the climate history of the region	
	~ 할 것 같다
summer monsoon	
	갑작스러운 변화
the amount of evaporation	
	강우를 초과하다
indicative of a drought	
the weakening of ~	
	지속하다
recover to the previous conditions	

Paragraph F

it has long been thought that ~	
Bronze Age civilisations	
	비슷한 시기에
a global-scale climate event	
being seen as the cause	
local-scale processes	
the real archaeological interest	
lie in understanding	
the vast area of ~	
variable weather systems	
essential	
obtain more climate data	
	~에 가까운

Paragraph G

	~에 대한 세부 사항들
how people led their lives	
analyse grains cultivated at the time	
work out whether ~	
under extreme conditions of water stress	
adjust the combinations of crops	
look at whether ~	
the types of pottery	
other aspects of their material culture	
be distinctive to ~	
give us insight into	
	상호적인 관계
	~에 관여하다(참여하다)

Paragraph H

be in a unique position	특별한 위치에 있다
	조사하다
respond to ~	~에 대해 반응하다
environmental pressure and threats	
engage with the public	
	관련된
administrative bodies	
proactive in issues	
such as ~	
the management and administration	
	도시와 시골 발전의 균형
	문화유산을 보호하다

TEST

4

Cutty Sark: the fastest sailing ship of all time

VOCA

Paragraph 1

great technological development	대단한 기술적 발전
the major changes	주요한 변화
from A to B	A로부터 B
steam power	증기 동력
iron and steel	철과 강철

Paragraph 2

commercial sailing vessel	상업용 범선
clipper	쾌속 범선
three-mastered ships	돛대가 3개인 범선
transport	운송하다
take passengers	승객을 태우다
Suez Canal	수에즈 운하
steam propulsion	증기 추진
replace	대체하다
dominate world trade	세계의 무역을 지배하다
although	비록 ~이지만
survive	생존하다
more or less intact	다소 손상되지 않은
on display	전시 중

Paragraph 3

unusual name	독특한 이름
come from poem	시에서 들여오다
be chased by a witch	마녀에 의해 쫓기다
cutty sark	짧은 여성용 옷
a short nightdress	짧은 잠옷
be depicted in ~	~에 그려지다
forehead	앞면
the carving of women	여자의 조각

in legend	전설상
cross water	물을 건너다
a rather strange choice of ~	~에 대한 다소 이상한 선택

Paragraph 4

a shipping company owned by ~	~에 의해 소유된 운송회사
carry out construction	건설을 수행하다(하다)
a shipbuilding firm	조선 회사
ensure	보장하다, 확보하다
the contract with ~	~와의 계약
put A in B	A를 B에 놓다
in the end	결국, 마침내
be forced out of business	폐업하다
a competitor	경쟁자

Paragraph 5

active	적극적인
both profits and prestige	이익과 명성 둘 다
be designed to ~	~ 하도록 고안되다
make journey more quickly	항해를 더 빠르게 만들다
on her maiden voyage	처녀 항해에서
set sail	출항하다
carry large amounts of goods	많은 양의 물품을 운송하다
return laden with tea	차를 싣고 돌아오다
live up to ~	~의 기대에 부응하다
the high expectations of ~	~의 높은 기대
as a result of ~	~의 결과로
various misfortunes	다양한 불운들
on one occasion	한번은, 언젠가
gain a lead	선두에 나서다
rudder	키
be severely damaged	심각하게 손상되다
in stormy seas	폭풍의 바다
make A impossible to steer	A를 불가능하게 하다
steer	조종하다
crew	선원
the daunting task	힘든 일
repair	수리하다
succeed at the second attempt	두 번째 시도에서 성공하다

Paragraph 6

pose a growing threat to ~	~에 증가하는 위협을 가하다
cargo capacity	화물 적재량
in addition	덧붙여서
launch	출항하다
have a serious impact	중대한 영향을 주다
steam ships	(증기로 움직이는) 기선, 상선
make use of ~	~을 이용하다
Mediterranean and Red Sea	지중해와 홍해(*수에즈 운하에 의해 연결됨)
be of no use	유용하지 않다
sail a far greater distance	더 먼 거리를 항해하다
reduce the journey time	항해 시간을 줄이다
by approximately two months	대략 두 달 차이

Paragraph 7

be interested in ~	~에 관심이 있다
instead	대신에
take on	떠맡다
much less prestigious work	훨씬 덜 가치 있는 일
carry cargo	화물을 운송하다
violence aboard the ship	선상에서의 폭력
lead ultimately to	궁극적으로 초래하다
the replacement of the captain	선장의 교체
an incompetent drunkard	무능력한 술고래
steal the crew's wages	선원들의 급여를 훔치다
be suspended from ~	~로부터 금지당하다
appoint	지명하다, 정하다
mark a turnaround	전환점이 되다
beat	물리치다
by around a month	약 한 달의 차이

Paragraph 8

an excellent navigator	우수한 항해사
get the best out of ~	~을 최대한 활용하다
depend on ~	~에 좌우되다
strong trade winds	강한 무역풍
the southern hemisphere	남반구
dangerously close to icebergs	위험하게 빙산에 가깝게
his gamble paid off	그의 도박은 성공했다

Paragraph 9

competition	경쟁
approach	다가오다, 도달하다
life expectancy	수명
become less profitable	덜 이익이 되다
be sold to ~	~에게 팔려지다
rename	이름을 바꾸다
miscellaneous cargoes	갖가지 잡다한 화물들

Paragraph 10

badly damaged in a gale	심하게 돌풍에 손상된
be put into harbor	항구에 놓이다
a retired sea captain	은퇴한 선장
determine	결정하다
return to ~	~로 돌아가다
the following year	다음해

Paragraph 11

no longer ~	더 이상 ~ 않다
be transferred to ~	~로 옮겨지다
dry dock	물이 마른 부두
go on public display	공개 전시를 하다
suffer from fire	화재로 고통받다
attract	끌다
a quarter of ~	~의 4분의 1

REVIEW

Paragraph 1

great technological development	
	주요한 변화
	A로부터 B
steam power	
iron and steel	

Paragraph 2

commercial sailing vessel	
clipper	
three-mastered ships	
	운송하다
	승객을 태우다
Suez Canal	
steam propulsion	
	대체하다
dominate world trade	
	비록 ~이지만
	생존하다
	다소 손상되지 않은
	전시 중

Paragraph 3

	독특한 이름
come from poem	
be chased by a witch	
cutty sark	
a short nightdress	
be depicted in ~	
forehead	
the carving of women	
	전설상
cross water	
a rather strange choice of ~	

Paragraph 4

a shipping company owned by ~	
carry out construction	
a shipbuilding firm	
	보장하다, 확보하다
	~와의 계약
	A를 B에 놓다
	결국, 마침내
be forced out of business	
	경쟁자

Paragraph 5

active	
both profits and prestige	
	~ 하도록 고안되다
	항해를 더 빠르게 만들다
on her maiden voyage	
set sail	
carry large amounts of goods	
return laden with tea	
	~의 기대에 부응하다
	~의 높은 기대
	~의 결과로
various misfortunes	
	한번은, 언젠가
gain a lead	
rudder	
be severely damaged	
in stormy seas	
make A impossible	
steer	
	선원
	힘든 일
	수리하다
succeed at the second attempt	

Paragraph 6

	~에 증가하는 위협을 가하다
	화물 적재량
	덧붙여서
	출항하다
	중대한 영향을 주다
steam ships	
	~을 이용하다
Mediterranean and Red Sea	
	유용하지 않다
sail a far greater distance	
reduce the journey time	
by approximately two months	

Paragraph 7

	~에 관심이 있다
	대신에
	떠맡다
much less prestigious work	
	화물을 운송하다
violence aboard the ship	
	궁극적으로 초래하다
the replacement of the captain	
an incompetent drunkard	
steal the crew's wages	
be suspended from ~	
	지명하다, 정하다
	전환점이 되다
	물리치다
by around a month	

Paragraph 8

	우수한 항해사
get the best out of ~	
	~에 좌우되다
strong trade winds	
the southern hemisphere	
dangerously close to icebergs	
	그의 도박은 성공했다

Paragraph 9

	경쟁
	다가오다, 도달하다
	수명
	덜 이익이 되다
	~에게 팔려지다
rename	
miscellaneous cargoes	

Paragraph 10

badly damaged in a gale	
be put into harbor	
a retired sea captain	
	결정하다
return to ~	
	다음해

Paragraph 11

	더 이상 ~ 않다
	~로 옮겨지다
dry dock	
	공개 전시를 하다
	화재로 고통받다
	끄다
	~의 4분의 1

PASSAGE 2
SAVING THE SOIL

VOCA

more than a third of ~	~의 3분의 1 이상
the Earth's top layer	지각의 최상층
be at risk	위험하다
precious resource	귀중한 자원

Paragraph A

soil	토양
be endangered	위험에 처하다
according to ~	~에 따르면
slow the decline	감소를 늦추다
all farmable soil	모든 농사 가능한 토양
sustain	지탱하게 하다
in other more surprising way	다른 더 놀라운 방법에 있어서
a huge problem	큰 문제

Paragraph B

institute	연구소
point out	주장하다, 강조하다
warn about ~	~에 대해 경고하다
the degradation of ~	~의 악화
for decades	수십 년 동안
at the same time	동시에
contain	포함하다
B as well as A	A뿐만 아니라 B도
microorganisms	미생물들
such as viruses and fungi	바이러스와 균류
amid decomposing plants	부패 중인 식물 중에
various minerals	다양한 무기물들
not just A, but B	A뿐만 아니라 B도
the source of ~	~의 원천
existing antibiotics	기존 항생제들
in the fight against ~	~의 퇴치에 있어서

antibiotic resistant bacteria	항생제 내성균
an ally against climate change	기후 변화에 대항하는 동지
digest	먹다, 소화하다
lock in	가두다, 감금하다
carbon content	탄소 함유량
the amount of carbon	탄소의 양
the entire atmosphere	전체 대기
store	저장하다
prevent flood damage	홍수의 피해를 막다
damage to ~	~에 대한 손상
caused by ~	~에 의해 야기된
cost	비용이 들다

Paragraph C

lose its ability	그의 능력을 잃다
perform functions	기능들을 수행하다
the human race	인류
be in big trouble	큰 곤란에 처하다
disappear completely	완전히 사라지다
special property	특별한 특성
will be lost	사라질 것이다
once ~	일단 ~ 하면
it may takes A thousands of years	A가 수천 년이 걸릴 수도 있다
recover	회복하다
agriculture	농업
by far the biggest	훨씬 가장 큰
in the wild	야생에서
remove nutrients	영양분을 제거하다
die and decay	죽고 부패하다
return to the soil	토양으로 돌아가다
tend not to ~	~ 하지 않는 경향이 있다
return A to B	A를 B로 돌려주다
unused parts of harvested crops	수확된 작물의 미사용 부분
enrich	비옥화하다
become less fertile	덜 비옥하게 되다
in the past	과거에는
develop strategy	전략을 개발하다
get around the problem	문제를 해결하다(극복하다)
varying the types	형태를 다양화시키는 것
leaving field uncultivated	토지를 경작하지 않는 상태로 놔두는 것

Paragraph D

practice	실행, 관행
become inconvenient	알맞지 않게 되다
as population grow	인구가 증가함에 따라
be run	운영되다
on more commercial lines	더 상업적인 노선에서
manufacture ammonium nitrate	질산암모늄을 만들다
put A on B	A를 B에 넣다
synthetic fertiliser	합성 비료
ever since	그 후 줄곧
over the past few decades	지난 수십 년에 걸쳐서
such a bright idea	그러한 긍정적인 생각
chemical fertilisers	화학 비료
release A into B	A에 B를 방출하다
polluting nitrous oxide	오염 질소
the atmosphere	대기
excess	과잉, 초과
be washed away	씻겨 나가다
more recently	더 최근에
indiscriminate use of fertilisers	비료의 무절제 사용
hurt the soil itself	토양 그 자체를 손상시키다
turn it acidic and salty	그것을 산성 및 염분으로 바꾸다
degrade the soil	토양을 악화시키다
be supposed to nourish	영양분을 공급해야 한다

Paragraph E

look for	찾다
a solution to ~	~에 대한 해법
start out	시작하다
run a tree-care business	나무 돌봄 사업을 운영하다
advise	조언하다
came to realize	깨닫게 되다
ensure	확실하게 하다, 보장하다
flourish	번창하다
take care of ~	~을 돌보다
develop a cocktail of ~	~의 혼합제를 개발하다
fungi and humus	균류와 부엽토
by years of fertiliser overuse	수년의 과도한 비료 사용에 의해
apply A to B	A를 B에 적용하다

desert-like test plots	사막 같은 테스트 대지(터)
emerged	나타난
at the surface	표면에서
roots strong enough	충분히 강한 뿌리들
pierce dirt	흙을 뚫다
as hard as rock	바위만큼 단단한
fed with ~	~이 공급된/제공된

Paragraph F

measures like this	이와 같은 조치들은
solve	해결하다
assess options	선택들을 평가하다
on a global scale	세계적인 규모로
an accurate picture	정확한 파악
face	직면하다
for one thing	한편으로는
there is no agreed international system	동의된 국제적인 체계가 없다
classify soil	토양을 분류하다
in an attempt to ~	~ 하려는 시도로
unify the different approaches	다른 접근법들을 단일화하다
work together	협력하다
create a map	지도를 만들다
linked to a database	데이터베이스에 관련된
can be fed	공급될 수 있다
measurements	조치들
field surveys / drone survey	현장 조사, 무인 비행기 조사
satellite imagery / lab analyses	위성 이미지, 실험실 분석
real-time date	실시간 정보
on the state of the soil	토양의 상태에 대한
aim to ~	~을 목표로 하다
worldwide	세계적인
map to a depth of ~	~의 깊이까지 지도를 그리다
the results	결과
freely accessible to all	자유롭게 모든 것에 접근 가능한

Paragraph G

present the problem	문제를 제시하다
policy-makers	정책 입안자들
and vice versa	반대의 경우도 마찬가지
colleagues	동료들

propose a goal	목표를 제안하다
zero net land degradation	순제로 토양 악화
carbon neutrality	탄소 중립
an easily understood target	쉽게 동의된 목표
shape expectations	기대를 형성하다
encourage action	행동을 장려하다
soils on the brink	파멸 직전의 토양
agitate for	~를 주장하다
the immediate creation of ~	~의 즉각적인 신설
protected zones	보호된 구역들
for endangered soils	위험에 처한 토양들을 위한
define	정의하다, 규정하다
conserve	보존하다, 보호하다
the greatest soil diversity	최상의 토양 다양성
be present	현존하다
unspoilt soils	황폐되지 않은 토양
a future benchmark of quality	품질에 대한 미래의 기준
whatever we do	우리가 무엇을 하든
take action	조치를 취하다

REVIEW

more than a third of ~	
the Earth's top layer	
	위험하다
	귀중한 자원

Paragraph A

	토양
	위험에 처하다
	~에 따르면
	감소를 늦추다
all farmable soil	
	지탱하게 하다
in other more surprising way	
	큰 문제

Paragraph B

	연구소
	주장하다, 강조하다
warn about ~	
	~의 악화
	수십 년 동안
	동시에
	포함하다
	A뿐만 아니라 B도
microorganisms	
such as viruses and fungi	
amid decomposing plants	
various minerals	
	A뿐만 아니라 B도
the source of ~	
existing antibiotics	
in the fight against ~	
antibiotic resistant bacteria	
an ally against climate change	
	먹다, 소화하다
lock in	
carbon content	

the amount of carbon	
	전체 대기
	저장하다
prevent flood damage	
	~에 대한 손상
	~에 의해 야기된
	비용이 들다

Paragraph C

	그의 능력을 잃다
	기능들을 수행하다
	인류
	큰 곤란에 처하다
	완전히 사라지다
	특별한 특성
	사라질 것이다
	일단 ~ 하면
it may takes A thousands of years	
	회복하다
	농업
	훨씬 가장 큰
	야생에서
	영양분을 제거하다
	죽고 부패하다
	토양으로 돌아가다
tend not to ~	
return A to B	
unused parts of harvested crops	
	비옥화하다
	덜 비옥하게 되다
	과거에는
	전략을 개발하다
get around the problem	
varying the types	
leaving field uncultivated	

Paragraph D

	실행, 관행
	알맞지 않게 되다
	인구가 증가함에 따라

be run	
on more commercial lines	
manufacture ammonium nitrate	
put A on B	
synthetic fertiliser	
	그 후 줄곧
	지난 수십 년에 걸쳐서
	그러한 긍정적인 생각
	화학 비료
	A에 B를 방출하다
polluting nitrous oxide	
	대기
	과잉, 초과
be washed away	
	더 최근에
indiscriminate use of fertilisers	
hurt the soil itself	
turn it acidic and salty	
	토양을 악화시키다
be supposed to nourish	

Paragraph E

	찾다
	~에 대한 해법
	시작하다
run a tree-care business	
	조언하다
	깨닫게 되다
	확실하게 하다, 보장하다
	번창하다
	~을 돌보다
develop a cocktail of ~	
fungi and humus	
by years of fertiliser overuse	
	A를 B에 적용하다
desert-like test plots	
emerged	
at the surface	
roots strong enough	
pierce dirt	

as hard as rock	
fed with ~	

Paragraph F

	이와 같은 조치들은
	해결하다
	선택들을 평가하다
	세계적인 규모로
an accurate picture	
	직면하다
	한편으로는
there is no agreed international system	
	토양을 분류하다
	~ 하려는 시도로
unify the different approaches	
	협력하다
	지도를 만들다
linked to a database	
can be fed	
	조치들
field surveys / drone survey	
satellite imagery / lab analyses	
real-time date	
on the state of the soil	
	~을 목표로 하다
	세계적인
map to a depth of ~	
the results	
freely accessible to all	

Paragraph G

	문제를 제시하다
policy-makers	
and vice versa	
	동료들
propose a goal	
zero net land degradation	
carbon neutrality	
an easily understood target	
	기대를 형성하다

	행동을 장려하다
	파멸 직전의 토양
agitate for	
the immediate creation of ~	
protected zones	
for endangered soils	
	정의하다, 규정하다
	보존하다, 보호하다
the greatest soil diversity	
	현존하다
unspoilt soils	
a future benchmark of quality	
whatever we do	
	조치를 취하다

PASSAGE 3
Book Review

VOCA

Paragraph 1

the ultimate goal	궁극적인 목표
self-evidently good	증명할 필요 없이 좋은
matter	중요하다
give no further external reason	더 외부적인 이유를 제시하지 않다
obviously	분명하게
pronouncement	발표, 선언
an economist and advocate of ~	~의 경제학자와 지지자
positive psychology	긍정심리학
summarise	요약하다
the belief of ~	~에 대한 믿음
the purpose of ~	~에 대한 목적(의도)
promote	야기하다, 초래하다
a state of collective well-being	공동의 복지(행복) 상태
how to achieve it	그것을 성취하는 방법
a supposed science	추정(가정) 과학
not only A but also B	A뿐만 아니라 B도
what makes people happy	무엇이 사람을 행복하게 하는지
identify	밝히다, 확인하다
measure	측정하다
equipped with this science	과학을 갖춘
secure	보장하다, 확보하다

Paragraph 2

astonishingly crude	놀랍도록 있는 그대로의
simple-minded	순진한, 때 묻지 않은
be oblivious to ~	~을 염두에 두지 않다
the vast philosophical literature	거대한 철학 문학
be explored and questioned	탐구되고 질문되다
as if ~	마치 ~인 것처럼
on the subject	그 주제에 대해

philosopher	철학자
attention	관심
more than anyone else	다른 누구보다도
be responsible for ~	~에 대한 책임이 있다
this way of thinking	생각하는 방법
the human good	인간의 선(행복)
consist of ~	~로 구성되다
pleasure and the absence of pain	기쁨과 고통의 부재
identify A with B	A를 B로 밝히다(확인하다)
self-realisation	자기실현
thinkers	사색가들, 사상가들
through the ages	그 시대를 통해서
struggle to	애쓰다
reconcile A with B	A를 B와 일치시키다
the pursuit of happiness	행복의 추구
human values	인간의 가치
metaphysics or fiction	형이상학 또는 허구
without knowing anything much of him	그에 대한 많은 것을 아는 것 없이
the school of moral theory	도덕적 이론의 학파
establish	설립하다
intellectual conviction illiterate	지적 신념 문외한
in the history of ~	~의 역사에 있어서
advocates	지지자들
follow in his tracks	선례를 따르다
in rejecting	거부하는 데 있어서
as ~	~로서
outmoded and irrelevant	시대에 뒤떨어지고 관련 없는
pretty much	거의
the entirety of ~	~의 전체
ethical reflection on ~	~에 대한 윤리적 성찰
to date	지금까지

Paragraph 3

note	언급하다
The Happiness Industry	행복 산업
view	관점
a way of limiting moral inquiry	도덕적 탐구를 제한하는 방법
one of the virtues of ~	~의 가치 중에 하나는
rich, lucid and arresting book	풍부한, 명료한 그리고 주의를 끄는 책
place A in B	A를 B에 놓다

the current cult of happiness	행복에 대한 현대 예찬
in a well-defined historical framework	잘 정의된 역사적인 틀에서
far more than a philosopher	철학자보다 훨씬 더
associate with ~	~와 관련된
a public sector management consultant	공공 부문 경영 컨설턴트
Home Office	영국 내무성
the departments of government	정부 부처
be linked together	서로 연결되다
a set of ~	일련의 ~
conversation tube	대화 터널
a printing device	인쇄 장치
produce unforgeable banknotes	위조 불가 지폐들을 만들다
draw up plans for ~	~을 위해 계획하다
frigidarium	냉욕장
keep provisions	식량을 보존하다
his celebrated design	그의 유명한 디자인
be known as ~	~로 알려지다
Panopticon	원형교도소
in solitary confinement	독방에서
be visible to guards	경비원에게 보여지다
at all times	항상
be adopted	채택되다
surprisingly	놀랍게도
discuss the fact	사실을 토론하다
not just A, but also B	A뿐만 아니라 B도
an instrument of control	통제의 도구
be applied to ~	~에 적용되다

Paragraph 4

a pioneer of ~	~의 개척자
the science of happiness	행복의 과학
be regard as a science	과학으로 여겨지다
view A as B	A를 B로 보다
a complex of pleasurable sensations	즐거운 느낌의 복합체
be quantifies by ~	~에 의해 수량화되다
the human pulse rate	인간 맥박 수
alternatively	그 대신에
the standard for quantification	수량화를 위한 표준
claim	주장하다
the same quantity of pleasure	같은 기쁨의 양

consumer	소비자
be attracted by ~	~에 관심을 가지다, ~에 마음을 빼앗기다
the latter measure	후자 조치
associate A to B	A를 B에 연관 짓다
set the stage	단계를 정하다
the entangling of ~	~에 대한 얽힘
capitalism	자본주의
shape the business practices	비즈니스 관행을 형성하다

Paragraph 5

describe	묘사하다
the project of science of happiness	행복의 과학적인 연구(기획)
become integral to ~	~에 통합되다
redefine and treat	다시 정의하고 다루다
as psychological maladies	심리적 병폐로서
in addition	덧붙여서
pleasure and displeasure	즐거움과 불쾌
be objectively measured	객관적으로 측정되다
inform	정보를 제공하다, 알리다
management studies and advertising	경영 연구와 광고
the tendency of thinkers	사상가들의 경향
the founder of behaviourism	행동주의의 설립자
shape	형성하다
manipulate	조종하다
have no factural basis	사실적인 기반이 없다
become president of ~	~의 의장이 되다
be confined to experiments on ~	~에 대한 실험으로 한정하다
reductive model	감소하는(간단한) 방식
be applied	적용되다
become the goal of governments	정부의 목표가 되다
at minimum cost to ~	~에 대한 최저 비용으로
consider	고려하다
socially desirable ways	사회적으로 바람직한 방법들

Paragraph 6

modern industrial societies	현대 산업사회
appear to ~	~인 것 같다
the possibility of ~	~에 대한 가능성
ever-increasing happiness	계속 증가하는 행복
motivate	동기화하다

in their labours	그들의 노동에 있어서
whatever its intellectual pedigree	그의 지적 혈통(내력)이 무엇이든지
be a threat to ~	~에 대한 위협이다
human freedom	인간의 자유

REVIEW

Paragraph 1

	궁극적인 목표
self-evidently good	
	중요하다
give no further external reason	
	분명하게
	발표, 선언
an economist and advocate of ~	
	긍정심리학
	요약하다
	~에 대한 믿음
	~에 대한 목적(의도)
	야기하다, 초래하다
a state of collective well-being	
how to achieve it	
a supposed science	
	A뿐만 아니라 B도
what makes people happy	
	밝히다, 확인하다
	측정하다
equipped with this science	
	보장하다, 확보하다

Paragraph 2

astonishingly crude	
simple-minded	
be oblivious to ~	
the vast philosophical literature	
be explored and questioned	
	마치 ~인 것처럼
	그 주제에 대해
	철학자
	관심
more than anyone else	
	~에 대한 책임이 있다
this way of thinking	

the human good	
	~로 구성되다
pleasure and the absence of pain	
identify A with B	
	자기실현
	사색가들, 사상가들
	그 시대를 통해서
	~ 하려 애쓰다
reconcile A with B	
	행복의 추구
	인간의 가치
metaphysics or fiction	
without knowing anything much of him	
the school of moral theory	
	설립하다
intellectual conviction illiterate	지적 신념 문외한
	~의 역사에 있어서
advocates	
follow in his tracks	
in rejecting	
as ~	
outmoded and irrelevant	
pretty much	
the entirety of ~	
ethical reflection on ~	
	지금까지

Paragraph 3

	언급하다
The Happiness Industry	
	관점
a way of limiting moral inquiry	
one of the virtues of ~	
rich, lucid and arresting book	
	A를 B에 놓다
the current cult of happiness	
in a well-defined historical framework	
far more than a philosopher	
associate with ~	

a public sector management consultant	
Home Office	
the department of government	
	서로 연결되다
	일련의 ~
conversation tube	
a printing device	
	위조 불가 지폐들을 만들다
	~을 위해 계획하다
frigidarium	
	식량을 보존하다
his celebrated design	
	~로 알려지다
Panopticon	
	독방에서
be visible to guards	
	항상
	채택되다
	놀랍게도
	사실을 토론하다
	A뿐만 아니라 B도
an instrument of control	
	~에 적용되다

Paragraph 4

	~의 개척자
the science of happiness	
	과학으로 여겨지다
	A를 B로 보다
a complex of pleasurable sensations	
be quantifies by ~	
the human pulse rate	
	그 대신에
the standard for quantification	
	주장하다
the same quantity of pleasure	
	소비자
be attracted by ~	
the latter measure	
associate A to B	

set the stage	
the entangling of ~	
	자본주의
shape the business practices	

Paragraph 5

	묘사하다
the project of science of happiness	
	~에 통합되다
redefine and treat	
as psychological maladies	
	덧붙여서
	즐거움과 불쾌
	객관적으로 측정되다
	정보를 제공하다, 알리다
management studies and advertising	
	사상가들의 경향
the founder of behaviourism	
shape	형성하다
	조종하다
have no factural basis	
become president of ~	
be confined to experiments on ~	
reductive model	
	적용되다
become the goal of governments	
at minimum cost to ~	
	고려하다
socially desirable ways	

Paragraph 6

modern industrial societies	현대 산업사회
appear to ~	
	~에 대한 가능성
	계속 증가하는 행복
	동기화하다
in their labours	그들의 노동에 있어서
whatever its intellectual pedigree	
	~에 대한 위협이다
	인간의 자유